Adult Nonf
Y0-AHV-908
917.5904 CRIPPEN
Crippen, John
Visual explorer guide Florida
33410018129397   06-28-2022

VISUAL EXPLORER GUIDE
FLORIDA

VISUAL EXPLORER GUIDE
FLORIDA

JOHN CRIPPEN

amber
BOOKS

First published in 2022

Copyright © 2022 Amber Books Ltd

All rights reserved. No part of this publication may be reproduced, stored in a retrieval system, or transmitted in any form or by any means, electronic, mechanical, photocopying, recording, or otherwise, without prior written permission of the copyright holder.

Published by
Amber Books Ltd
United House
North Road
London
N7 9DP
United Kingdom
www.amberbooks.co.uk
Instagram: amberbooksltd
Facebook: amberbooks
Twitter: @amberbooks
Pinterest: amberbooksltd

Project Editor: Michael Spilling
Designer: Rick Fawcett
Picture Research: Terry Forshaw

ISBN: 978-1-83886-203-9

Printed in China

Contents

Introduction	6
Miami and the East Coast	8
Panhandle and the West Coast	68
Everglades and the Florida Keys	116
Orlando and Around	164
Picture credits	224

Introduction

Florida, officially nicknamed 'The Sunshine State', was the 27th state to enter the union, in 1845. Renowned for its beautiful weather, it is equally well known for being battered by powerful hurricanes with frightening regularity. This sort of seeming contradiction is reflected in other ways. Originally part of the frontier in the early 19th century (complete with Native American wars and massacres) and known for its exploitable natural resources (citrus, seafood and cattle grazing) it is now a world centre for modern tourism, with its theme parks and beaches. Known as 'god's waiting room' for the number of retirees that migrate there, it is also home to a youth culture that pioneered the giant student holiday parties known as 'spring break'. A true cultural and racial melting pot, it has its country style in the panhandle and its Hispanic influences in south and central Florida. It is the southernmost part of the continental United States and has large swathes of undeveloped land, but cities like Miami have the urbanity of places such as New York.

ABOVE:
Pelican boardwalk
Brown pelicans stroll along the boardwalk on Amelia Island.

OPPOSITE:
Dawn light
The sun rises over a pristine beach at Fort Lauderdale.

7

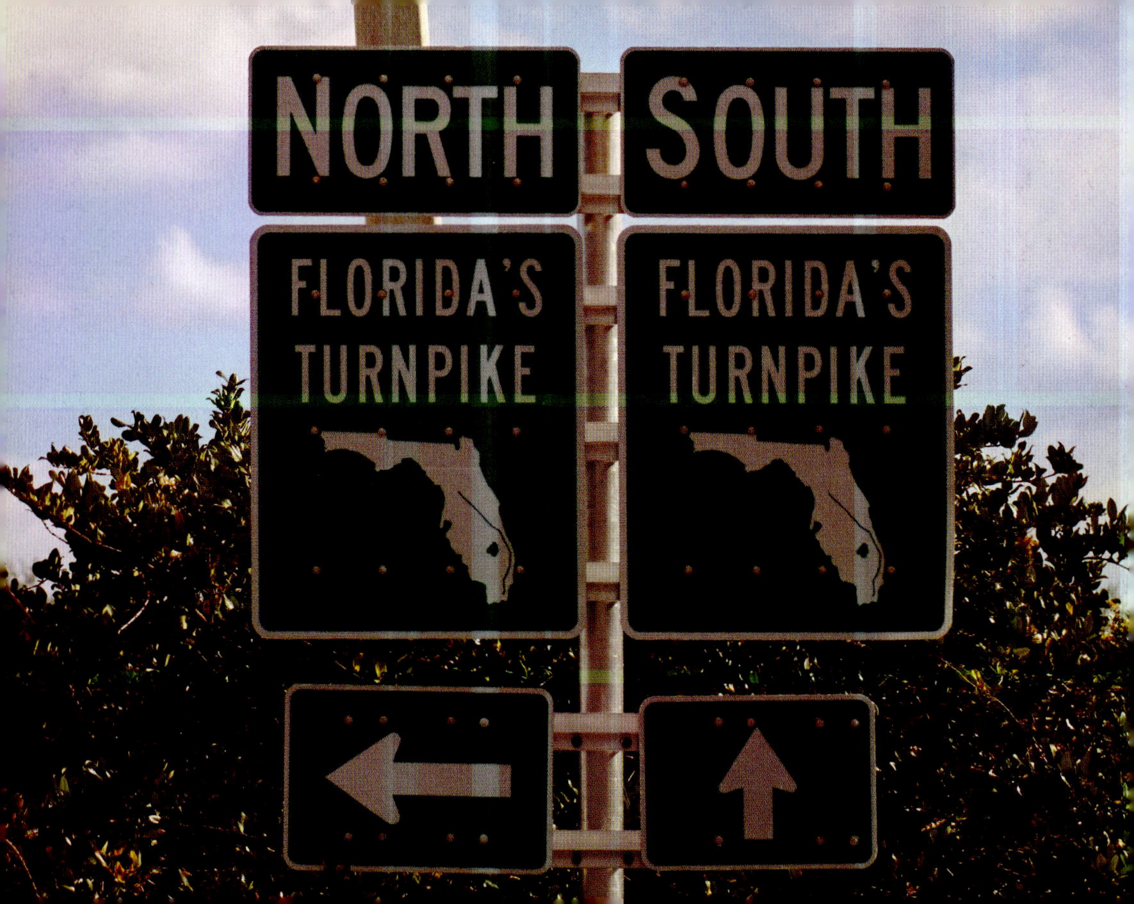
NORTH
SOUTH
FLORIDA'S TURNPIKE
FLORIDA'S TURNPIKE

Miami and the East Coast

Miami is the eighth-largest metropolitan area in the US and a major financial, commercial and cultural hub. It was home to the Tequesta, and possibly other Native American tribes, for some 2,000 years before European settlers moved in. Pedro Menendez de Aviles was the first governor and claimed the area for Spain in 1566. The area remained Spanish until Spain ceded it to the the United States in 1821. Miami became a city in 1896. Population growth was fueled by the 1920s land boom, but a huge hurricane in 1926 slowed this down. The Cuban revolution of 1959 spurred another influx and Little Havana became a Cuban enclave, which it remains. The drug problems of the 1980s, while doing little for the area's reputation, brought in lots of money and spurred growth in tourism and the hospitality sector.

Miami has the twelfth-largest urban economy in the US with a GDP of around $345 billion (about £259 billion), and it is the third richest city in the world (and second in the US) on purchasing power. Miami Beach is world famous and its success as a hotel and resort area is replicated all the way north to the Georgia state line, with many of those places having also found world recognition: Ft Lauderdale, Daytona, Clearwater, Palm Beach and St Petersburg, to name but a few. Florida's, and Miami's in particular, identity as the 'sunshine destination' for the northeastern part of the United States started in the 1920s and continues to this day.

OPPOSITE:
Florida Turnpike
The Florida Turnpike is the main artery connecting Central Florida to South Florida and Miami. It was opened in the 1950s.

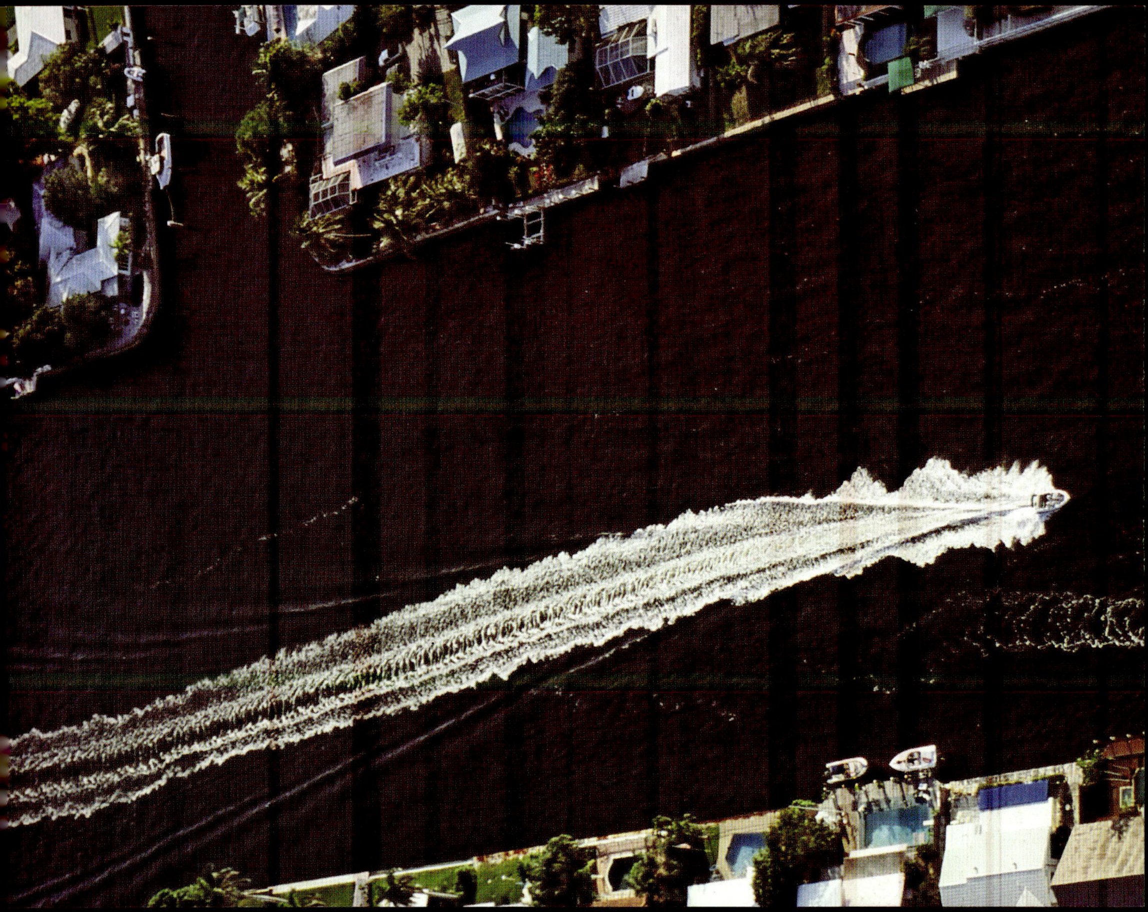

LEFT:

Speed boat, Miami
Miami is surrounded by the Caribbean Sea and the North Atlantic and its many waterways teem with craft of all sizes and purposes.

RIGHT:

St John's River, Jacksonville
For 10,000 years Floridians have lived for centuries along the St John's River. The first colony of settlers seeking religious freedom in the New World was founded on its shores in 1664. Jacksonville was founded at the foot of the river in 1822. During World War II, its shipyards supplied the Allies with shipping.

Jacksonville

On the coast of the St John's river, Jacksonville is major port, its deep water accommodating both military and commercial traffic. The Native American Timucua tribe were its original settlers before the French built Fort Caroline, a very early settlement, in 1564. The British followed and called the area Cow Ford and, after the US purchased it from the Spanish, it was named Jacksonville after President Andrew Jackson. Often battered by hurricanes and a victim of pollution related to urban sprawl, Jacksonville is now a thriving and vibrant modern community.

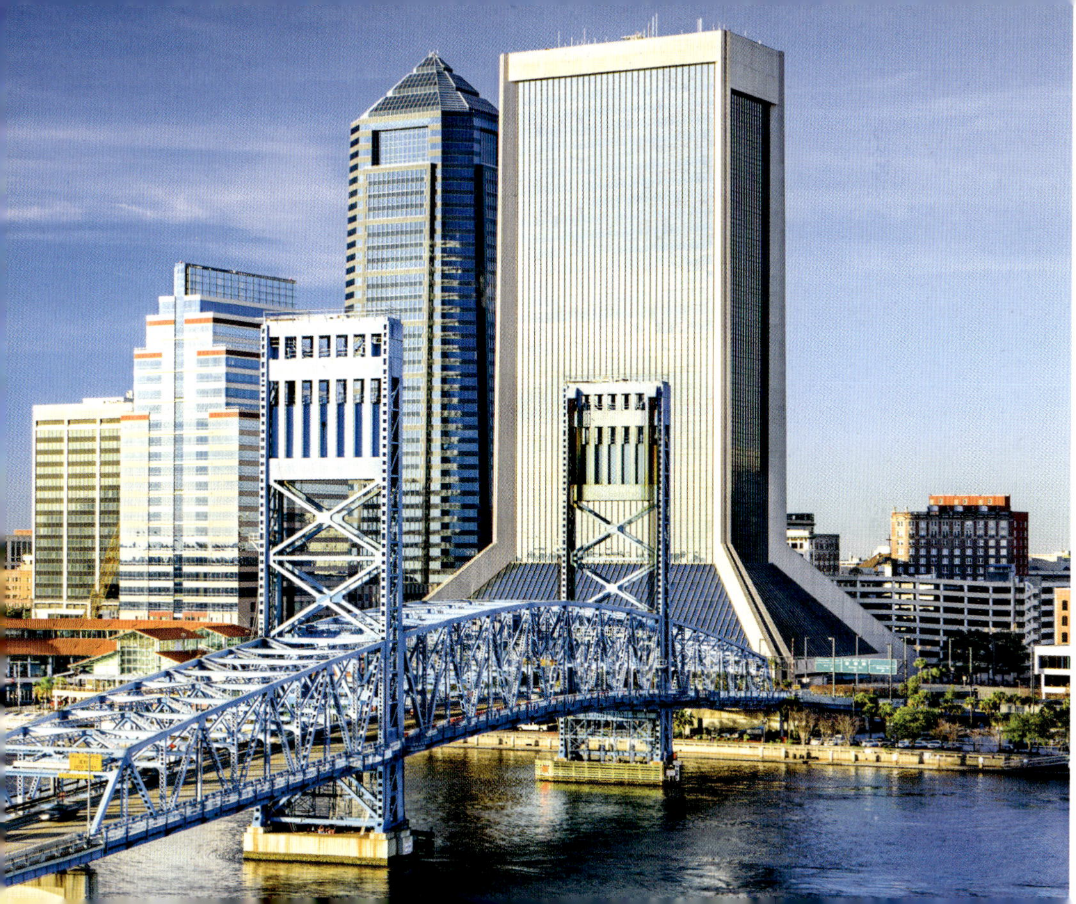

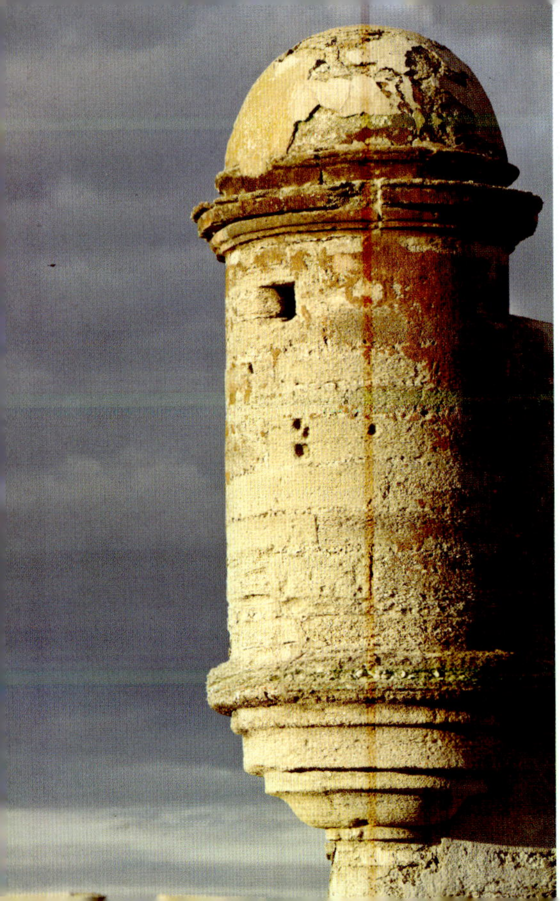
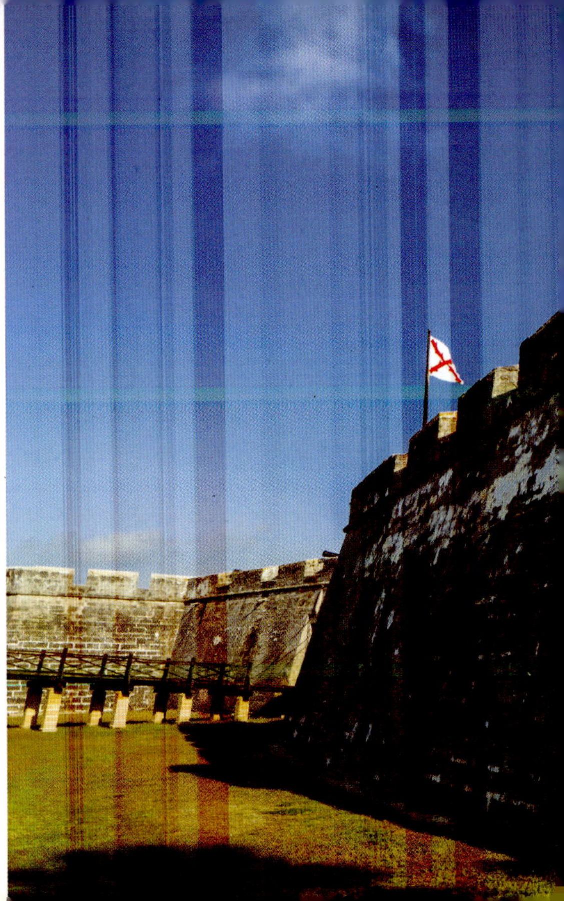

ALL PHOTOGRAPHS AND OVERLEAF:
Castillo de San Marcos This is the oldest masonry fort in the continental US. Declared a national monument in 1924, it was constructed by the Spanish in 1672 and has been used by Spanish, British and US forces, including the Civil War Confederacy, over its 251 years of military use. During the slave trade it was a port of embarkation for slaves sold by Britain to Spain, but then freed there. It was finally deactivated in 1933 and is now administered by the National Park Service.

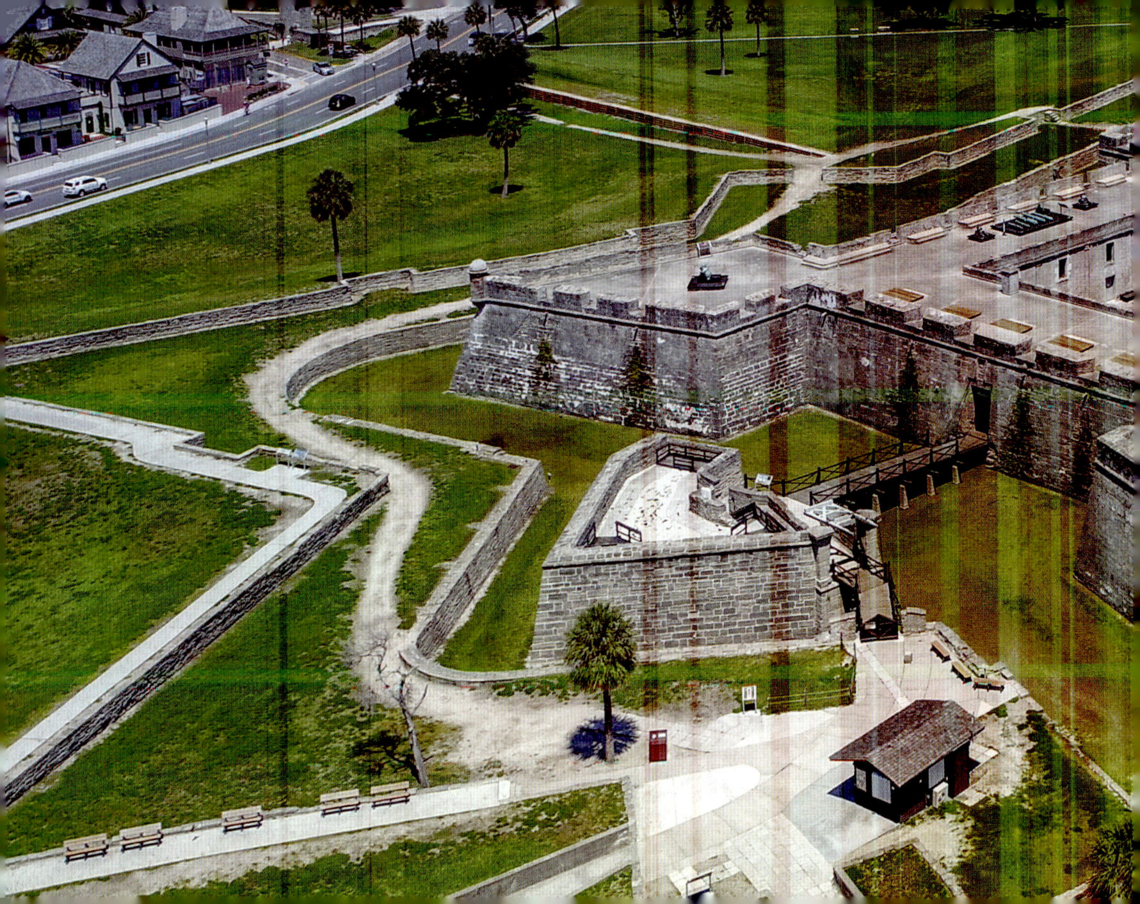

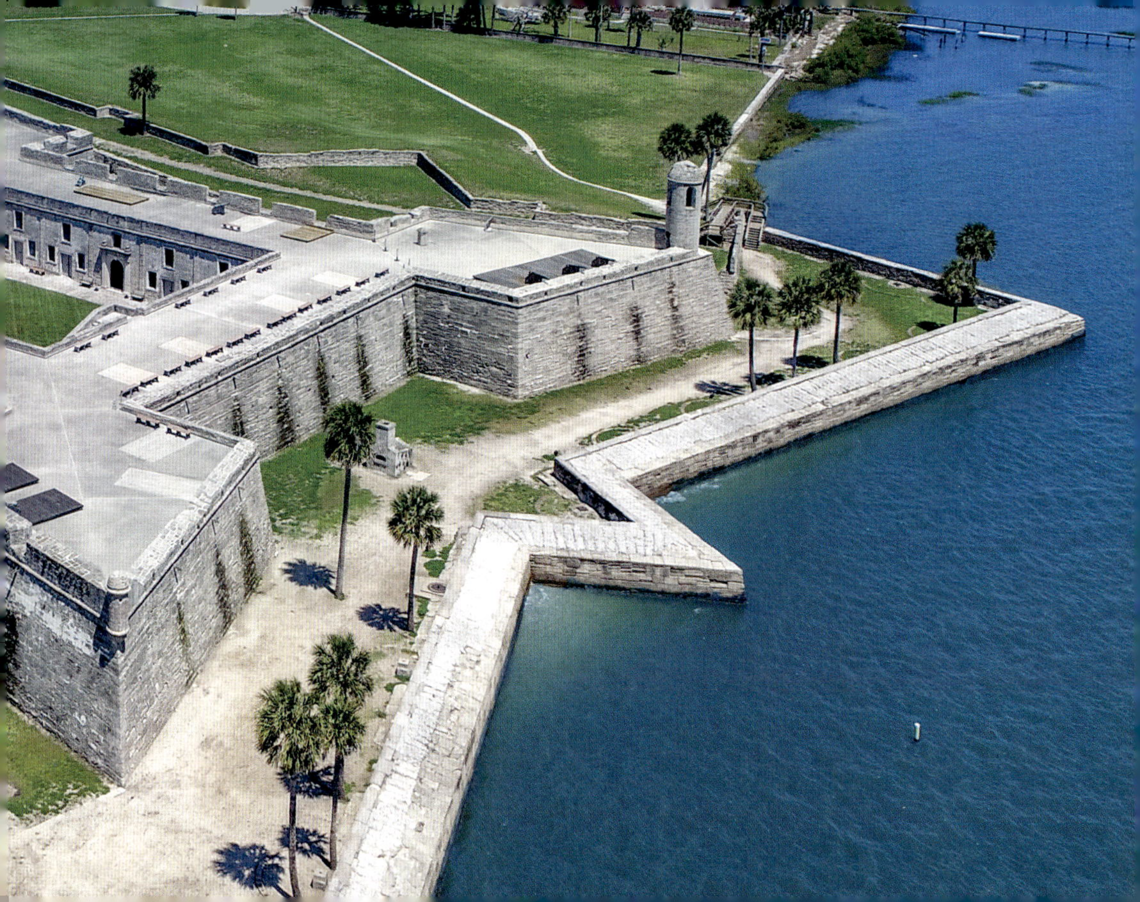

ABOVE:

St Augustine distillery
This locally owned and operated spirits distillery is housed in a late 19th-century ice plant and produces rum, bourbon, whiskey, gin and vodka from local produce.

RIGHT:

Bridge of Lions, St Augustine
Completed in 1927, the bridge, as much a work of art as a piece of infrastructure, was built during the land boom of the 20th century to allow cars to cross the intracoastal waterway.

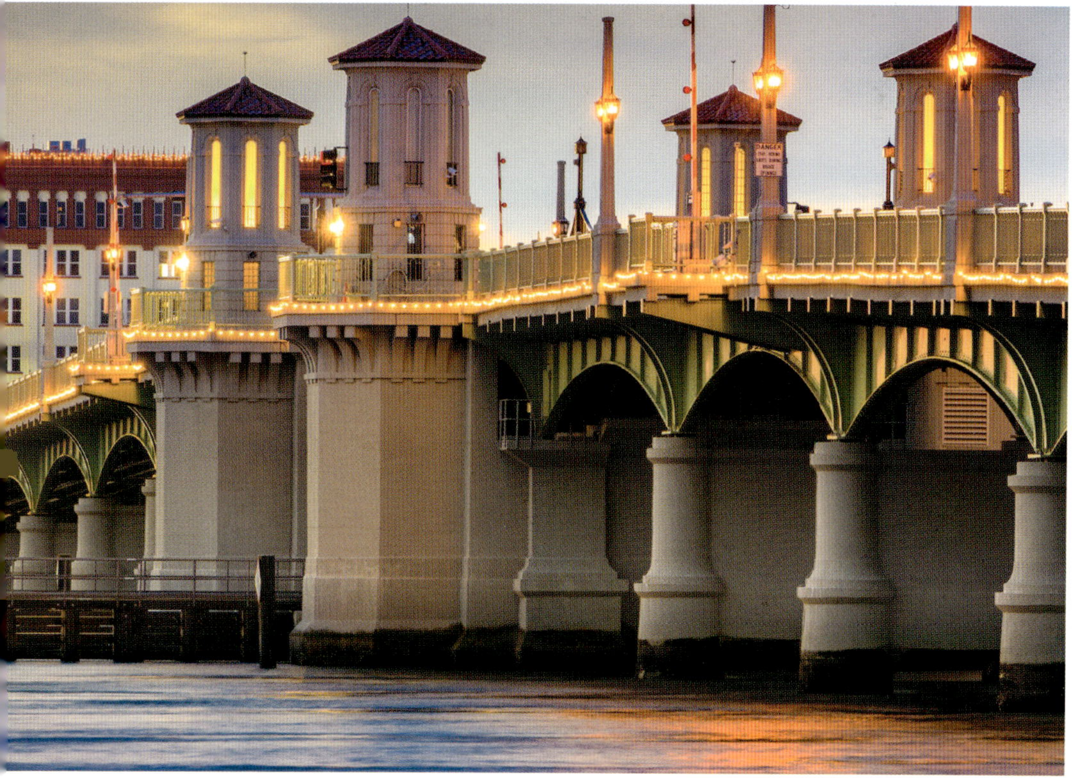
DANGER

ABOVE:
St Augustine Lighthouse
Privately owned and still working, this lighthouse was built between 1871–74.

RIGHT:
Snowy egret
This migratory bird, commonly found in Florida's wetlands, has has an average wingspan of 91cm (36in).

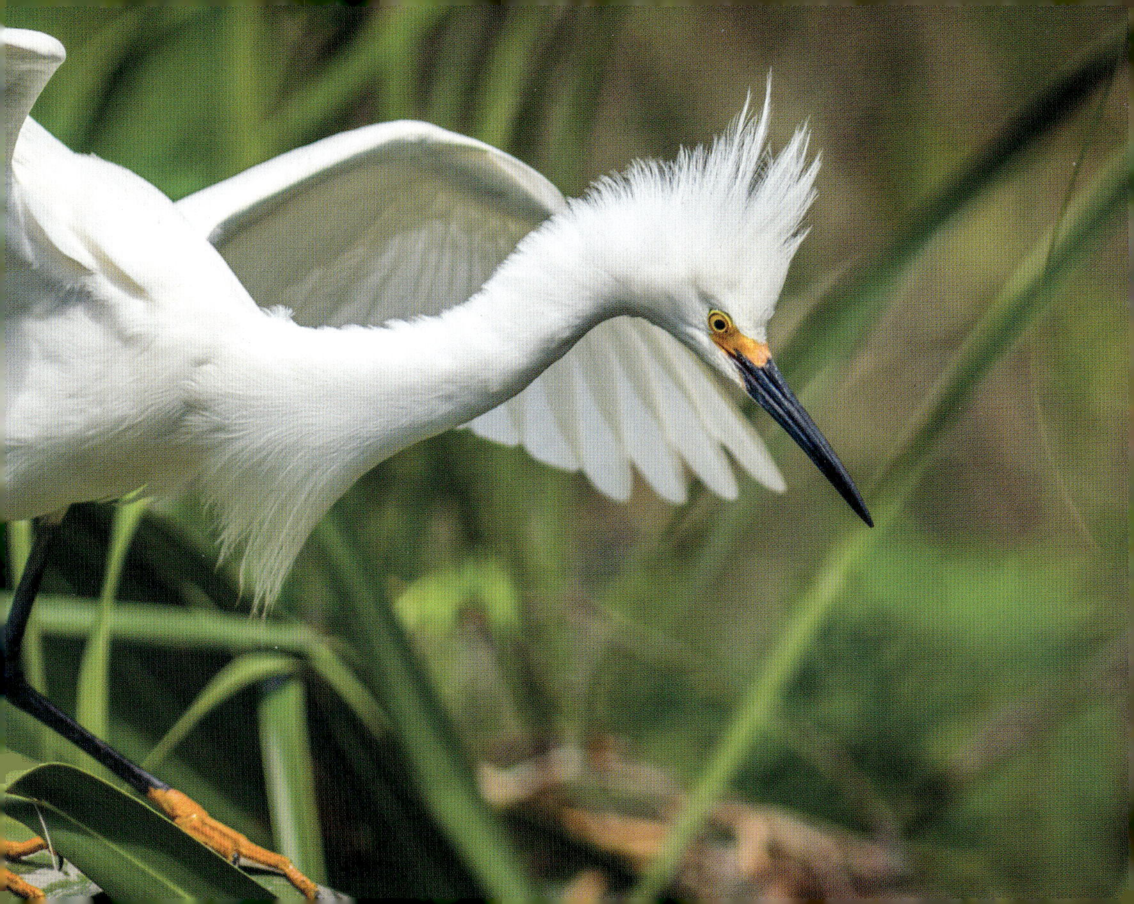

ALL PHOTOGRAPHS:
Daytona Beach
Known worldwide for its Speedway, Bike Week and the Daytona 500 stock car race, Daytona is also a top holiday destination. Visitors from all over the world join Floridians to enjoy the beach and the attendant 'honky tonk' culture, with its numerous bars and restaurants.

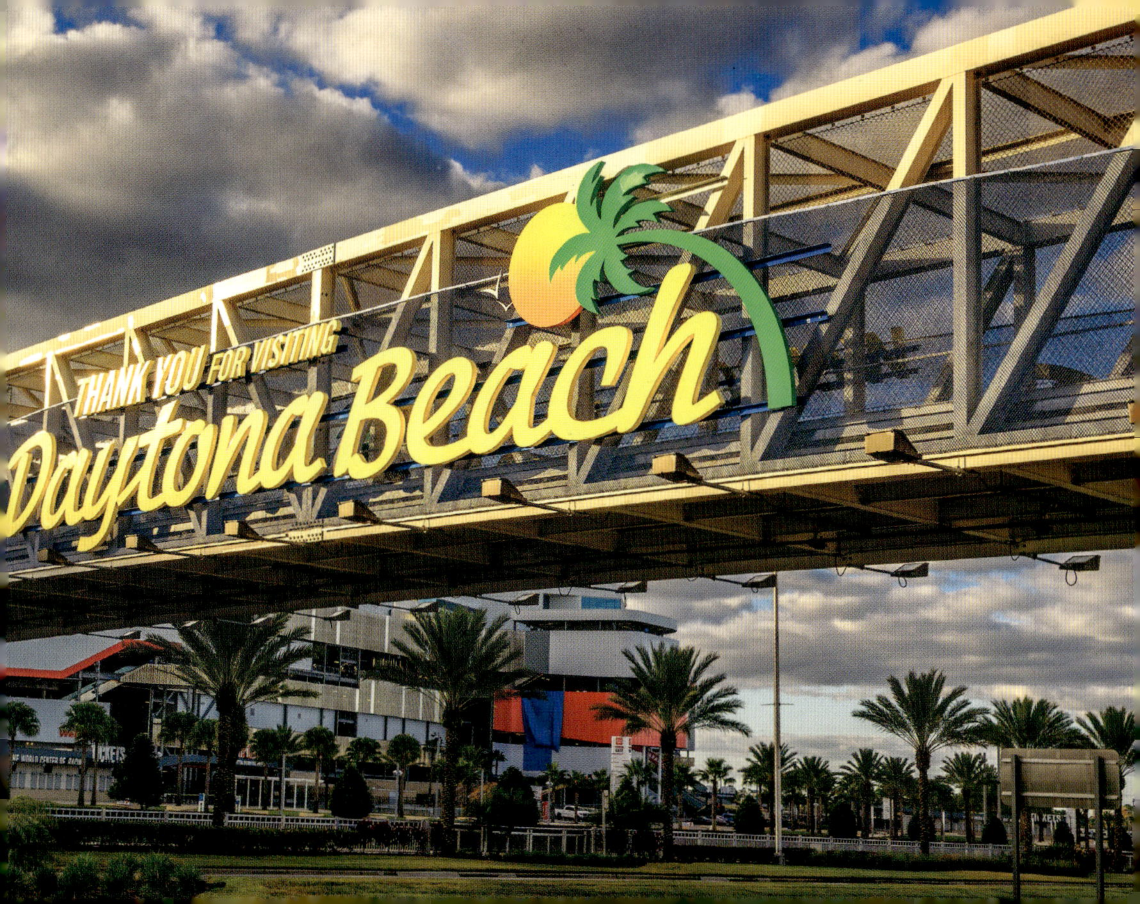
THANK YOU FOR VISITING
Daytona Beach

24

ALL PHOTOGRAPHS:
Daytona Beach
As well as its beach and pier, the town is known for Bike Week, which is usually held in the first full week in March, starting as just a race in 1932. Now it is a full week of events and draws huge crowds and a varied demographic from the very young to the very old. Thousands of motorcycles of all types and vintages parade through the town and the bars and restaurants are hopping. A second event, Biketoberfest, started in 1992 and is the autumn counterpart to spring's Bike Week.

OFFICIAL
253
BOWMAN
ally
BLANEY
BUESCHER
FASTENAL
TRUEX JR.
HARVICK
Mobil 1
KURT BUSCH
HAMLIN
KESELOWSKI
MUSTANG
LARSON
A. DILLON
DOW
LOGANO
PENNZOIL
ELLIOTT
BELL
Rheem
MUSTANG

ALL PHOTOGRAPHS:
Daytona 500 at the Daytona International Speedway
This 800km (500 mile) NASCAR series cup race was first held in 1959 and is the most important race on the NASCAR calendar, with the largest purse and the highest TV ratings. The track is 4km (2.5 miles), requiring 200 laps to complete the race. A second race, the Coke Zero 400, is also held annually here.

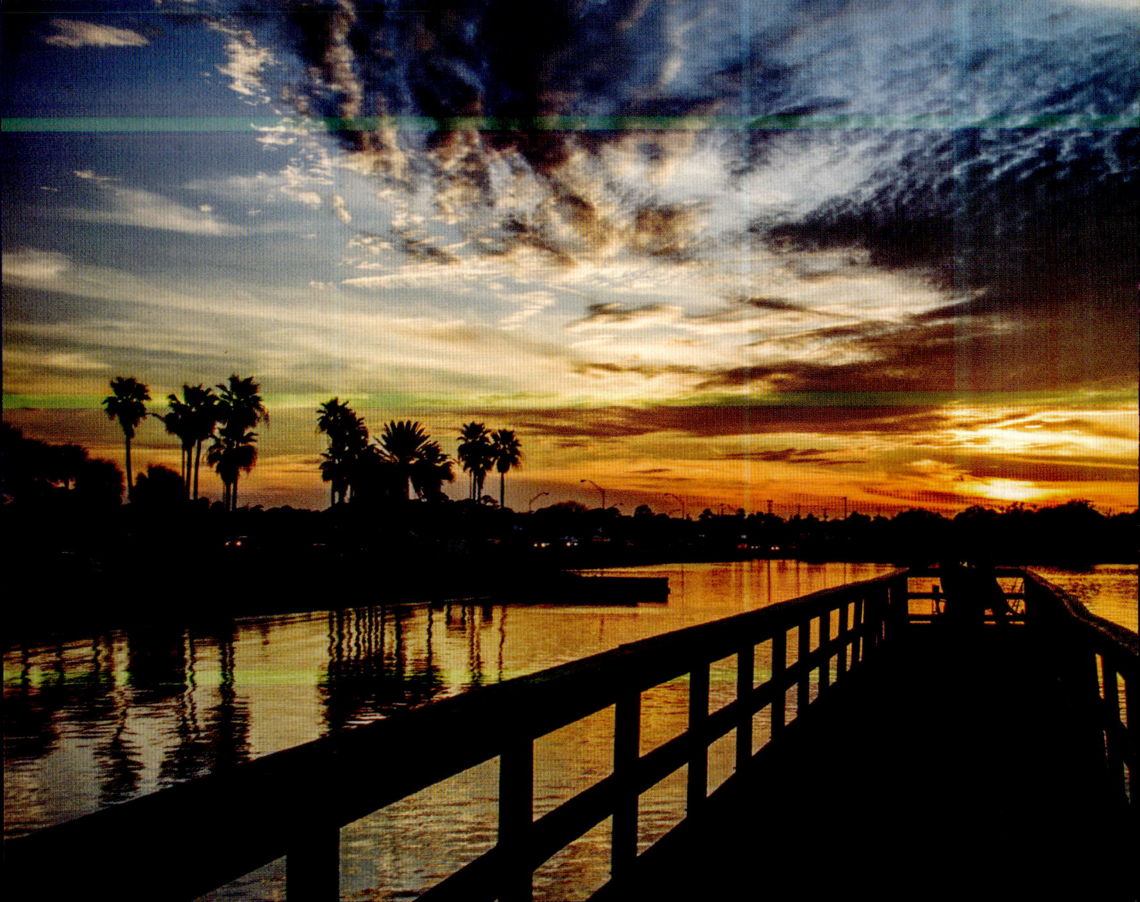

ALL PHOTOGRAPHS:
Port Orange
This spot is major player on the Fun Coast of Florida, along with Daytona Beach and Ormond Beach. The Last Resort (*pictured above*) was the hangout of Aileen Wuronos, the serial killer made famous by the film *Monster*. It has a Japanese garden with hanging motorcycles.

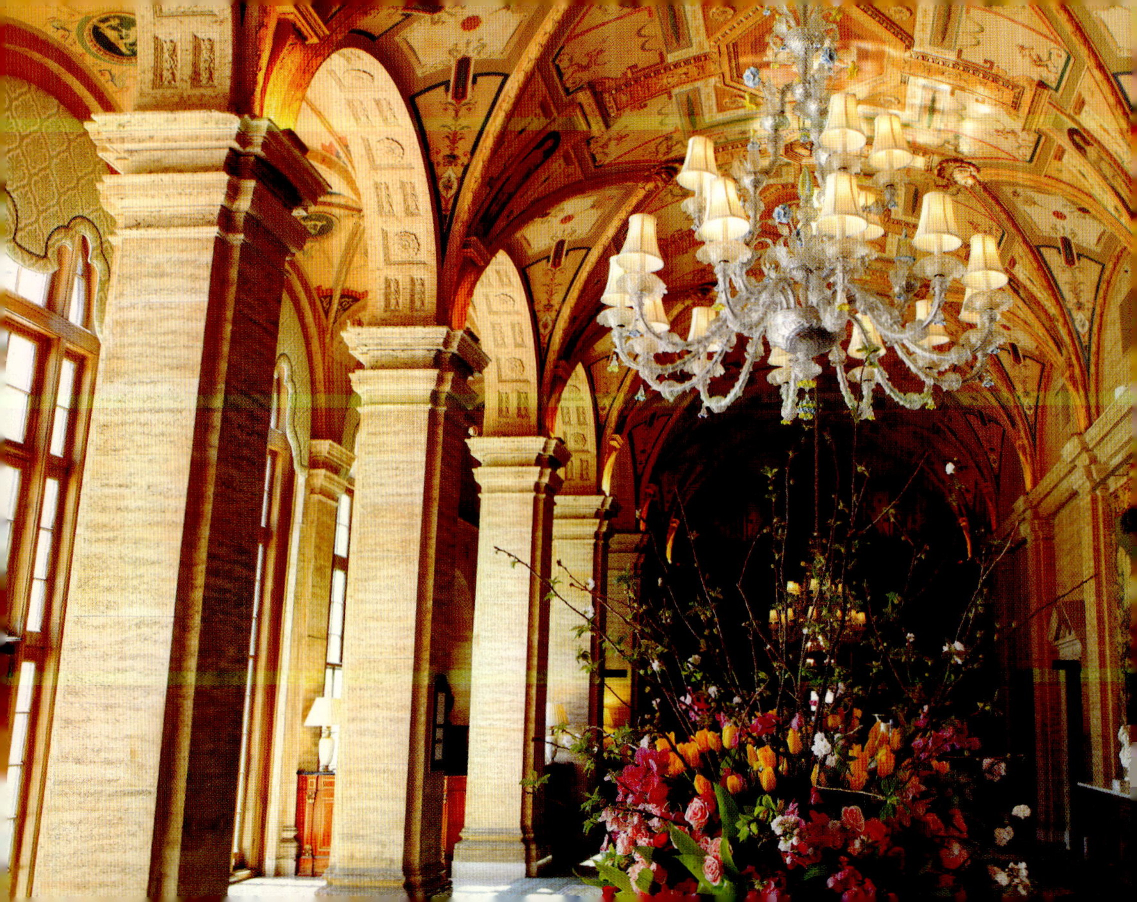

LEFT:
Breakers Hotel, Palm Beach
This luxury resort was built in the Italian Renaissance style in 1896 by Henry Morrison Flagler. Still owned by Flagler's descendants, it is known for its fine cuisine and even finer amenities.

ABOVE:
Memorial Horse Fountain, Town Hall, Palm Beach
Built by Addison Mizner in 1926, the building and small park are dedicated to Henry Morrison Flagler, whose hotels and railway pioneered the growth of South Florida in the early 20th century.

ABOVE:

Worth Avenue, Palm Beach

One of the most exclusive shopping areas in the world, this famous avenue featires designers as Givenchy and Valentino.

RIGHT:

State and County Fair, Palm Beach

Opening in 1912, the fair has been held in multiple different locations until 1958 when it moved to Palm Beach.

PIZZA
DRINKS • CALZONE • SOFT PRETZEL
RED VELVET
FUNNEL CAKES
ICE COLD DRINKS
OREO

ALL PHOTOGRAPHS:
Lake Worth Beach
Named after Lake Worth Lagoon, the city is now known as Lake Worth Beach. It has top tier beaches, a fishing pier, historic buildings and a newly revitalised downtown area with a pavement art festival, strolling musicians, and multiple ethnic festivals that reflect its diversity.

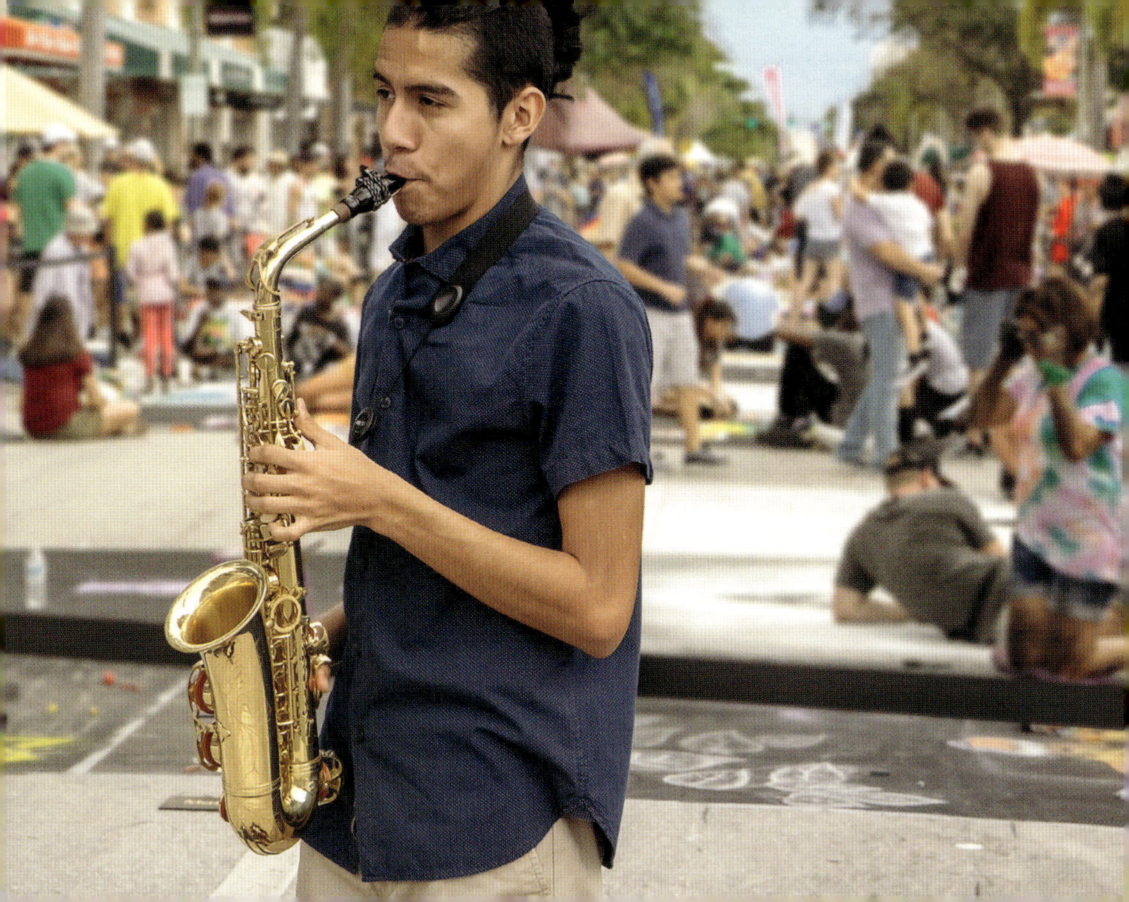

ALL PHOTOGRAPHS:
Deerfield Beach
Dating from 1890 and originally a farming community, the city has now become part of the Miami area. Known for its 1957 draw bridge, the city is also now home to a vibrant Brazilian and Haitian community.

Local musicians play the numerous festivals, as well as the pubs and bars of the area.

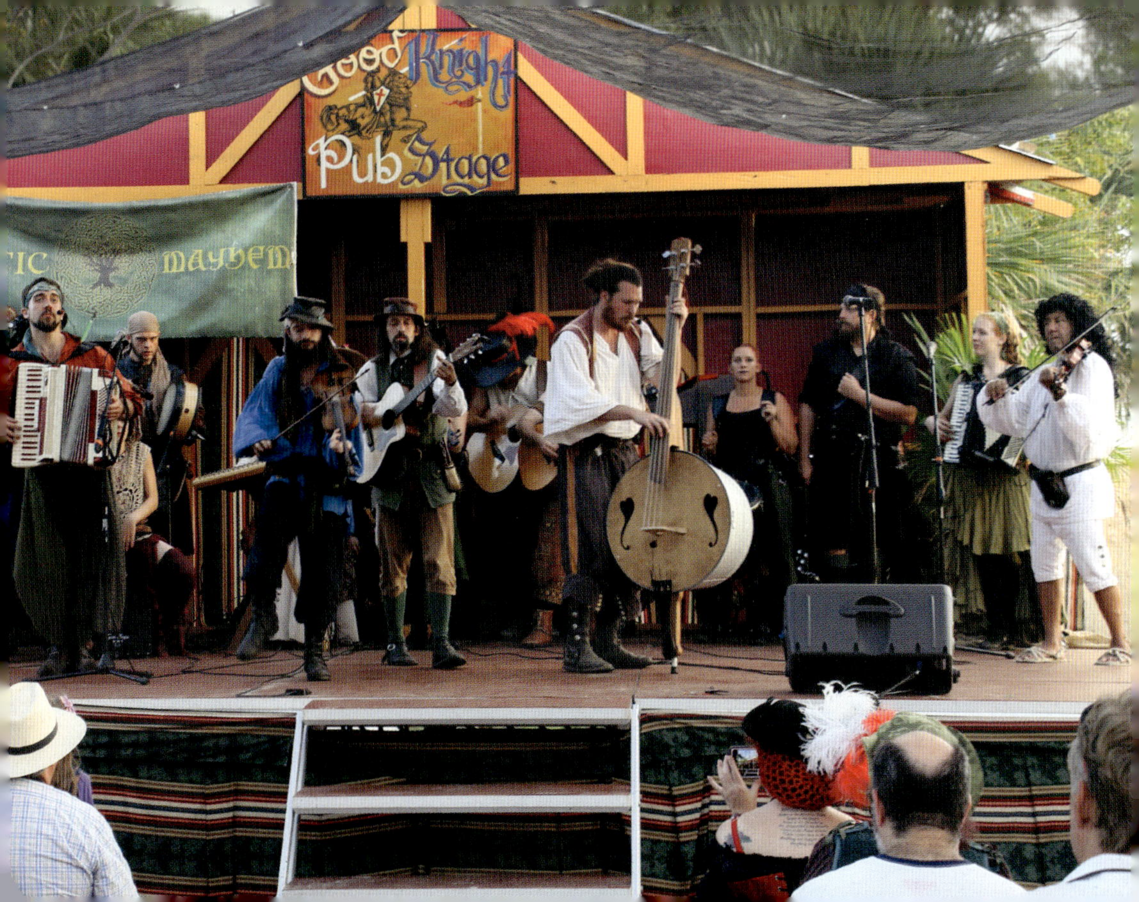

Good Knight
Pub Stage

RIGHT AND OPPOSITE:
River cruises, Fort Lauderdale
Featuring local scenery and wildlife, as well as the homes of the rich and famous, the many cruises available are a popular tourist activity.

BELOW:
South Broward, Fort Lauderdale
This area is famed for its al fresco waterfront restaurants and the relaxed lifestyle centered on the miles of coastline and waterways there.

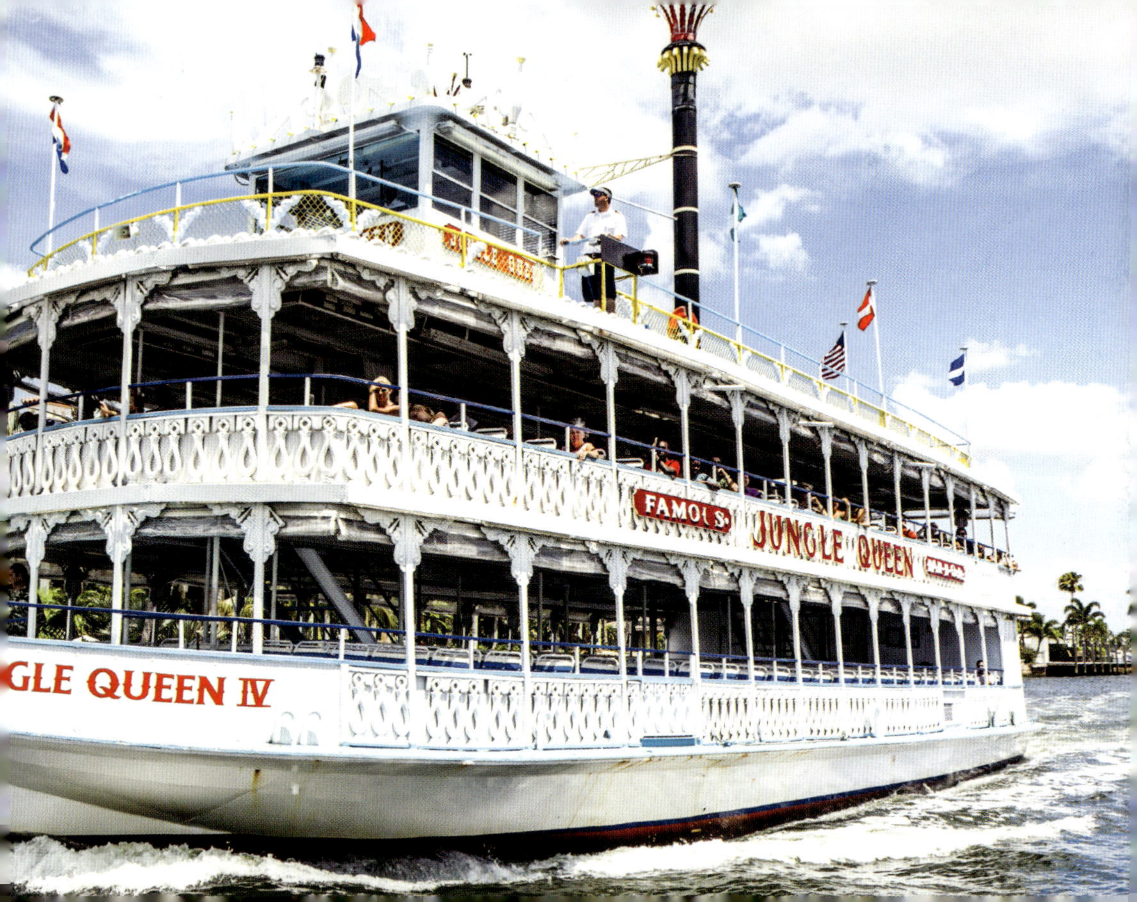

FAMOUS
JUNGLE QUEEN
GLE QUEEN IV

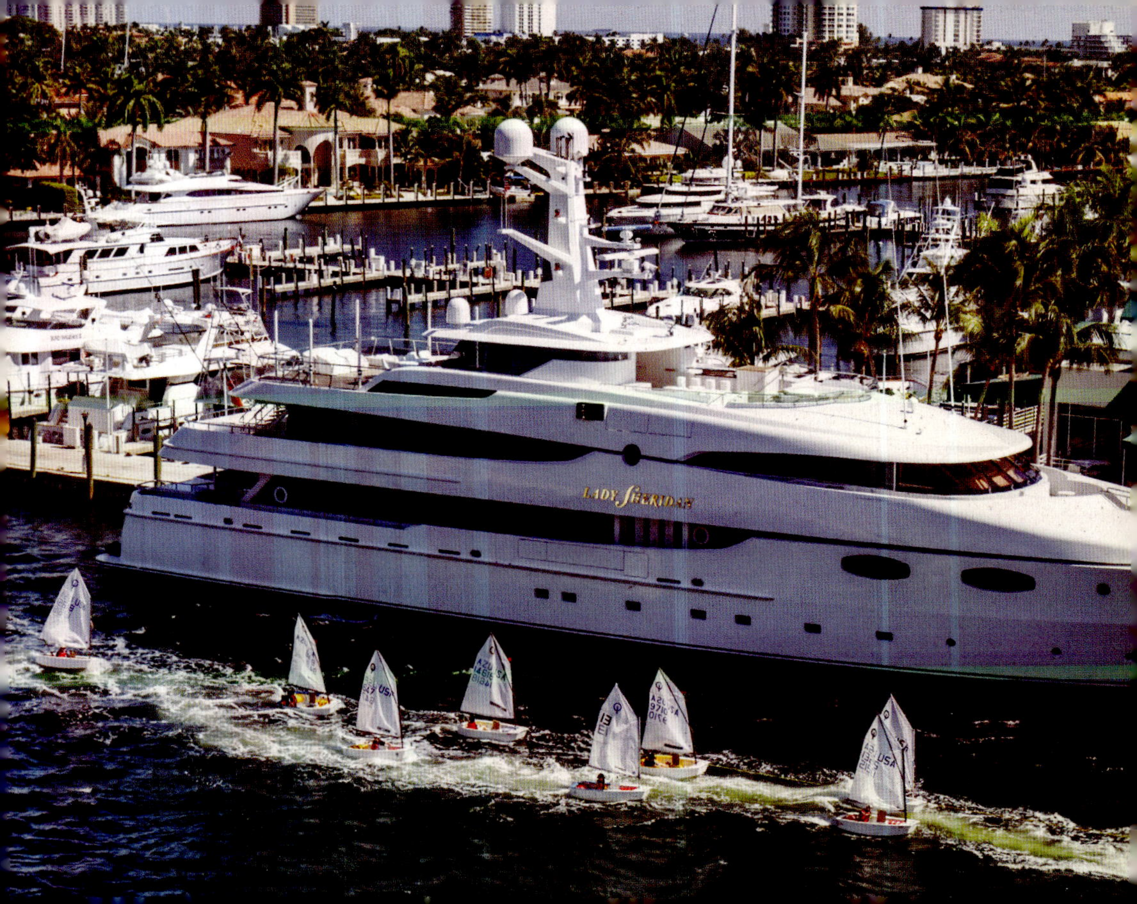
LADY SHERIDAN

ALL PHOTOGRAPHS:
Fort Lauderdale watersports
Fort Lauderdale is a major yachting locality, one of the nation's largest tourist destinations and a metropolitan division with 1.8 million people. The International Yacht Show has been running for over 50 years and marinas and boat dealers abound, as well as waterside restaurants, cafes and bars. You can buy your own, rent, or be taken on a cruise as you wish.

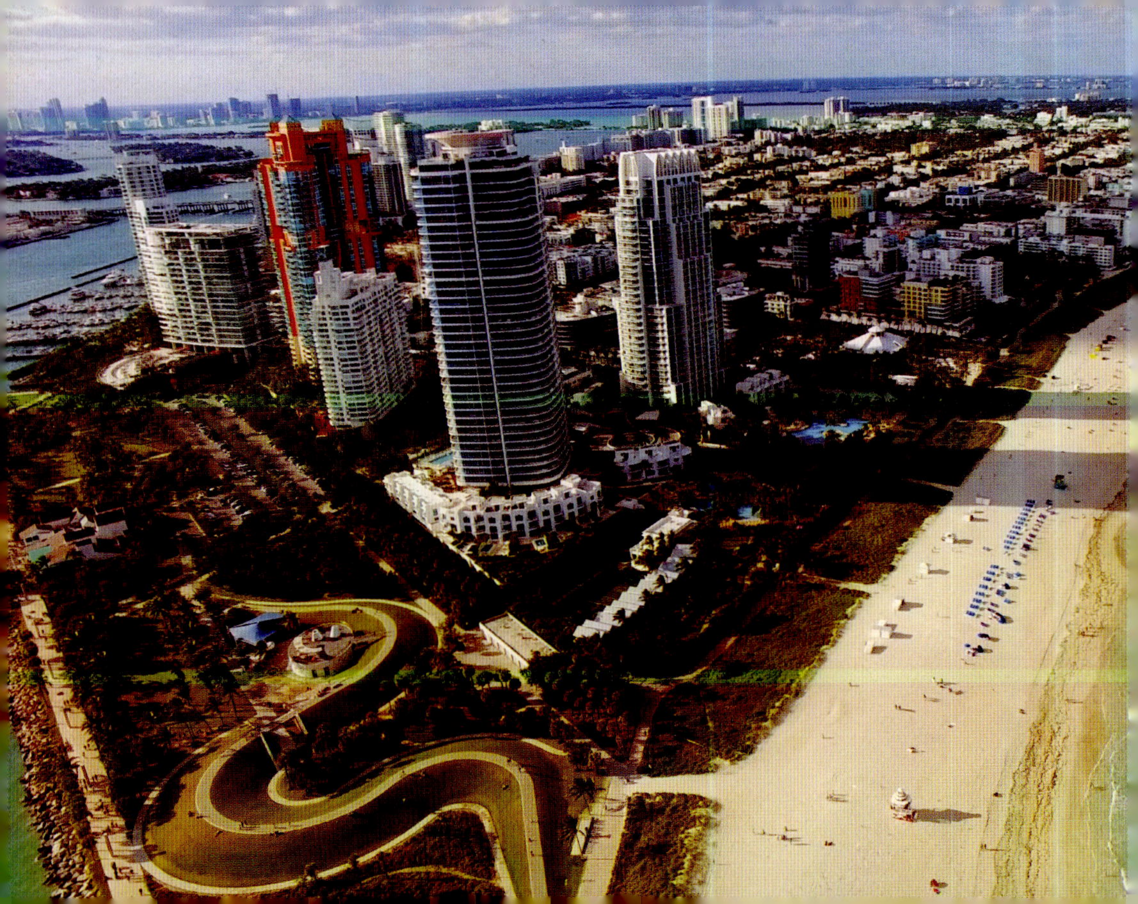

ALL PHOTOGRAPHS:
South Beach, Miami
The face of South Florida tourism since the 1920s, South Beach is familiar all over the world. The place that launched a million postcards, it is still a vibrant entertainment and leisure destination. The most expensive apartments can be found close to the beach.

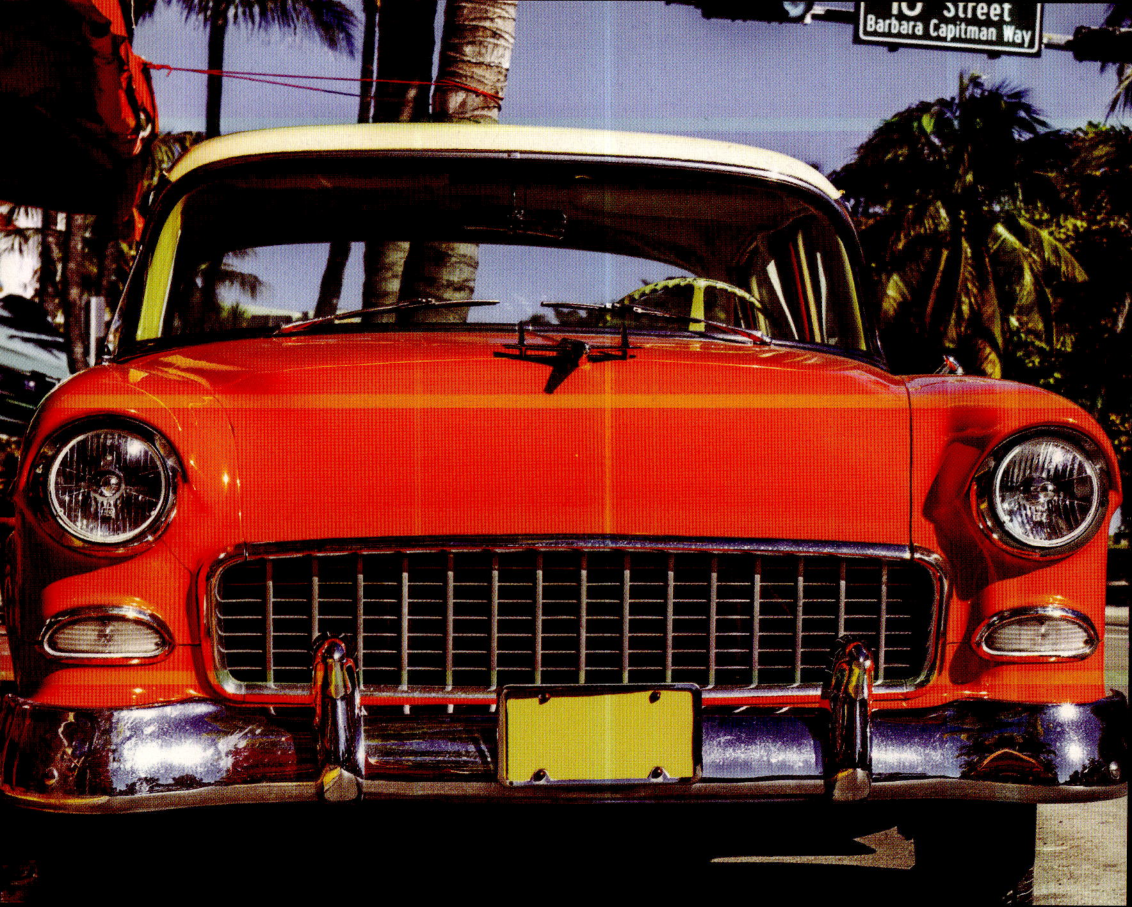
Street
Barbara Capitman Way

LEFT:
Vintage car, Ocean Drive, Miami
Popular as a regular ride and just for showing off, vintage cars are available in multiple dealerships. They can range from bangers to beauties.

ABOVE:
Colony Hotel, Miami
Recognised around the world as a symbol of the city, the Colony is an Art Deco treasure. It was designed by Henry Hohauser in 1935.

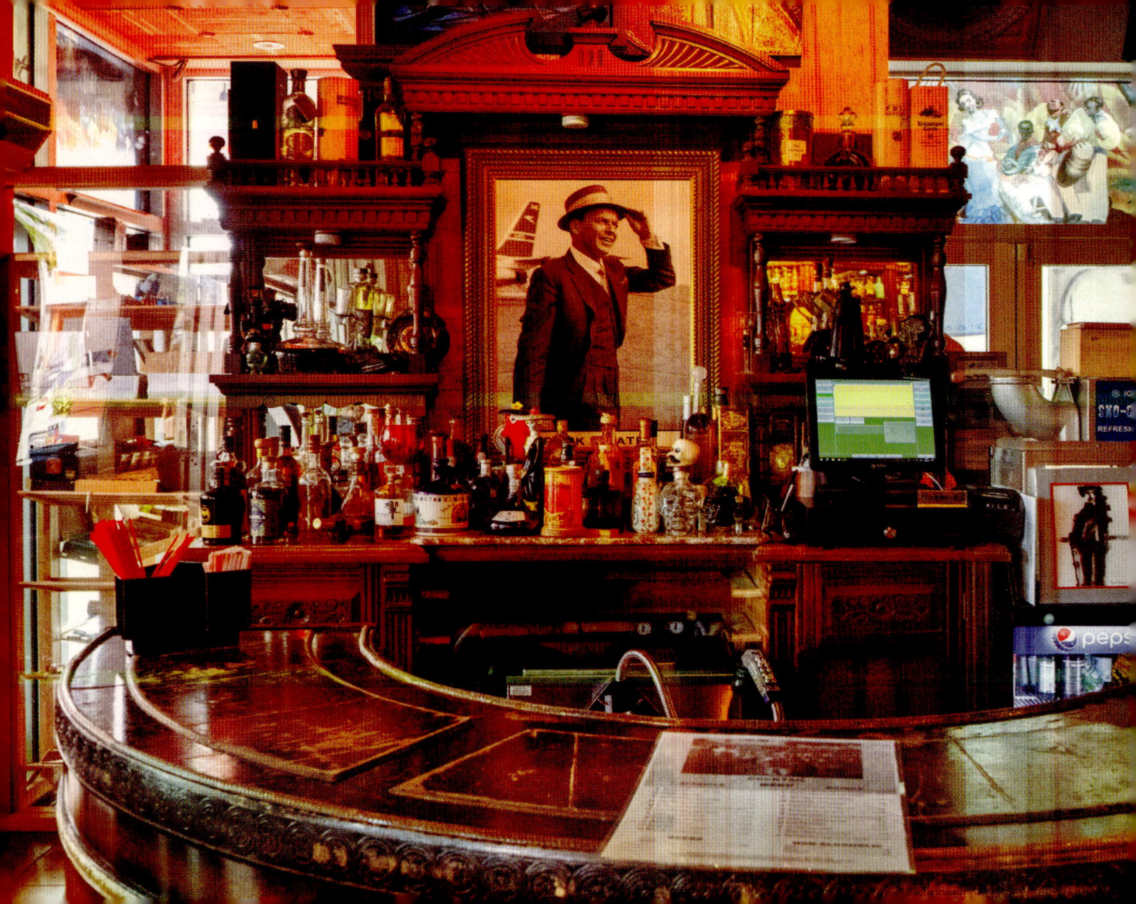

LEFT:

Cuba Ocho restaurant, Miami
This eatery houses 600 paintings, mostly Cuban art, collected by Roberto Rojas and displayed in the restaurant. He smuggled his first 14 paintings to the US in 1992 in a boat.

ABOVE:

Art Deco hotels, Miami
Originally built from 1915 through to the 1940s, and restored in the 1980s and 90s, these brightly painted hotels symbolise the city's past and are architectural gems. Most are found along Collins Avenue (named after Miami pioneer, John Collins) and also house cafes, restaurants and boutiques.

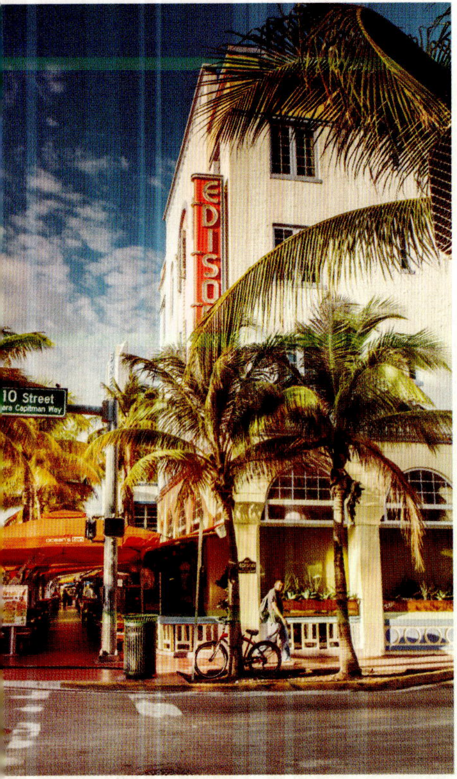
EDISO
10 Street

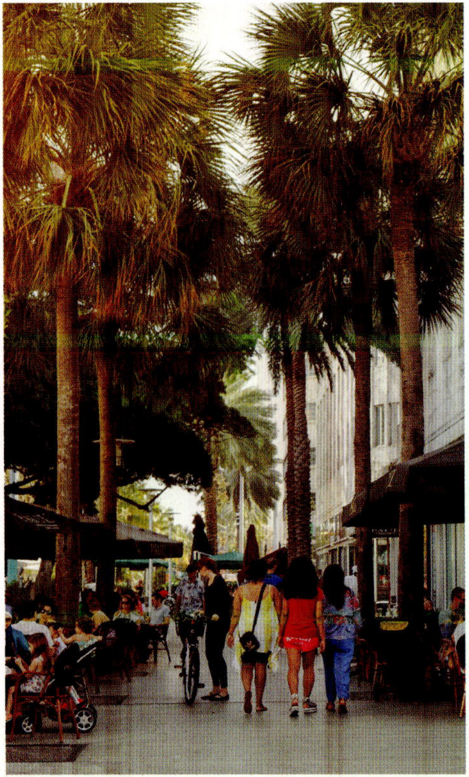

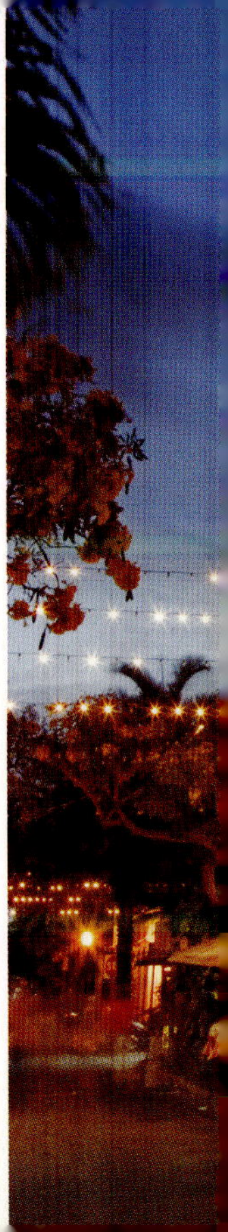

OPPOSITE LEFT:
**Ocean Drive,
South Beach, Miami**
Running parallel to the beach, this Miami's legedary strip and features beautiful Art Deco restaurants, bars and boutique hotels.

OPPOSITE RIGHT:
**Lincoln Road,
South Beach, Miami**
Dating back to 1912, Lincoln Road is a pedestrian shopping precinct with over 200 retailers and hotels, right off Ocean Drive.

LEFT:
**Espanola Way,
South Beach, Miami**
This Mediterranean-inspired area of shops, restaurants and hotels was originally planned as an artist's colony.

49

ALL PHOTOGRAPHS:
Little Havana, Miami
Originally a southern and Jewish district, the Cuban influx of the 1960s following Fidel Castro's revolution turned into Little Havana, a place to find the best coffee and Cuban food in the city. Chess players in Domino Park (*above*) carry on the tradition of Cuban world champion from 1920, Jose Raul Capablanca. Cigar-making still features in Little Havana, with lots of small factories turning out smokes for an international clientele, usually using closely guarded techniques.

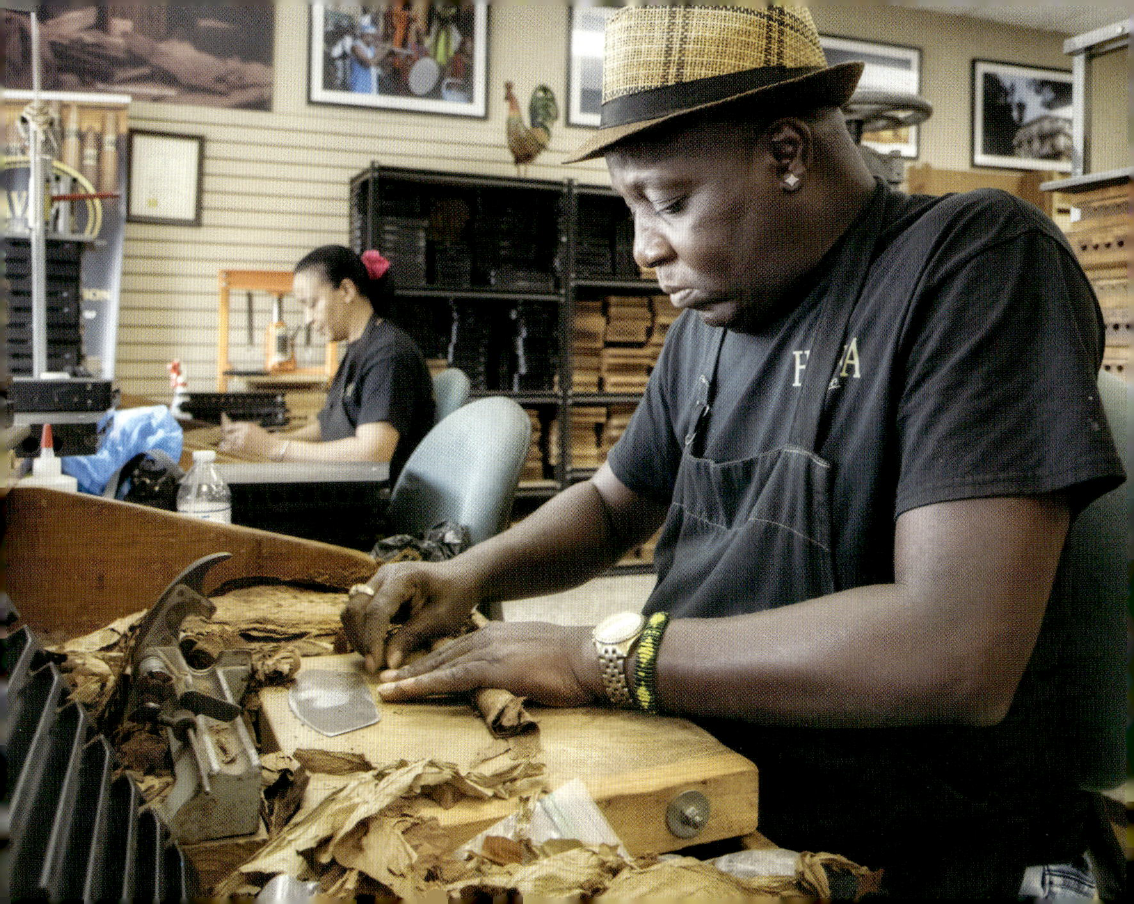

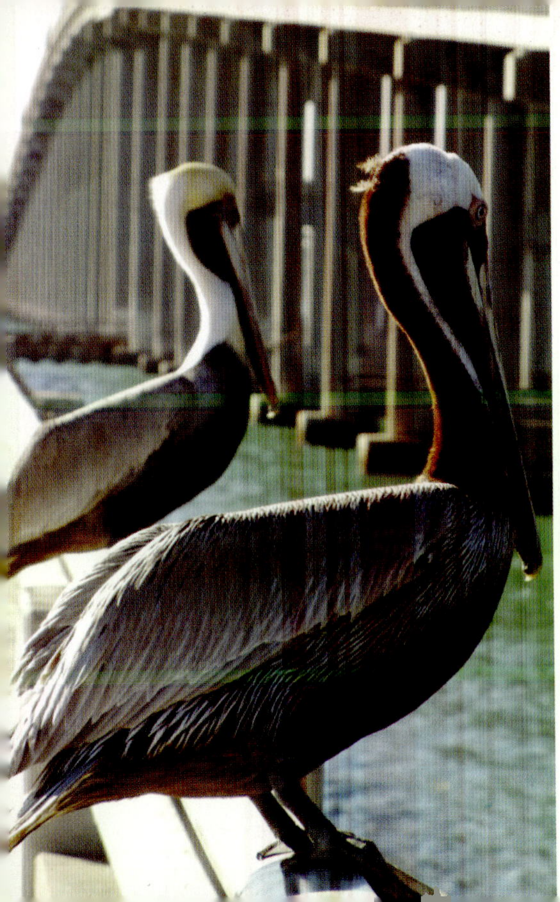
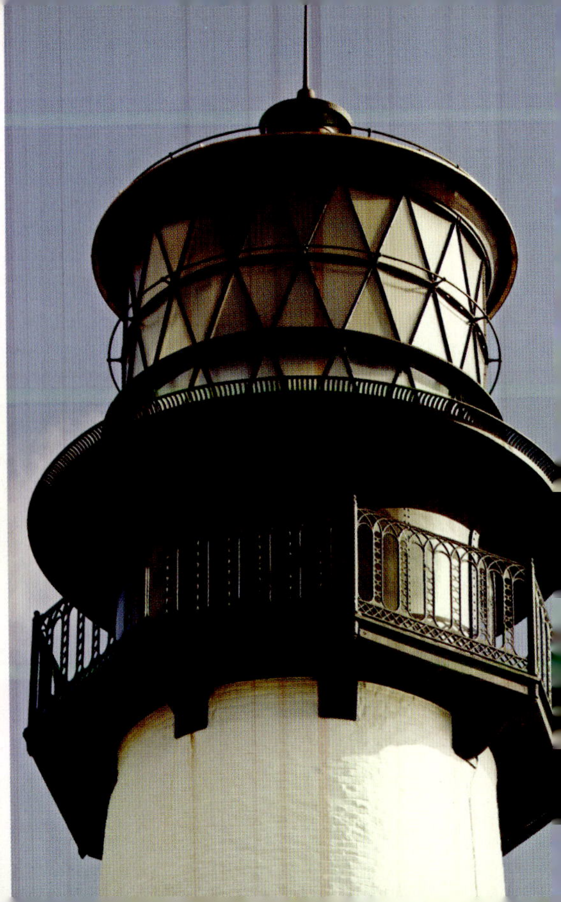

OPPOSITE:
Storks, Key Biscane Bridge
A modest fee allows you to go to the top of the bridge and see the great views of downtown and the port of Miami. The storks get it for free.

LEFT:
Cape Florida Lighthouse
This lighthouse is located in Bill Baggs Cape Florida State Park and is the oldest standing structure in Miami-Dade county, dating from 1825.

ABOVE:
Seafood, Key Biscane
The village of Key Biscayne, and the surrounding area, supports over 50 restaurants serving local seafood.

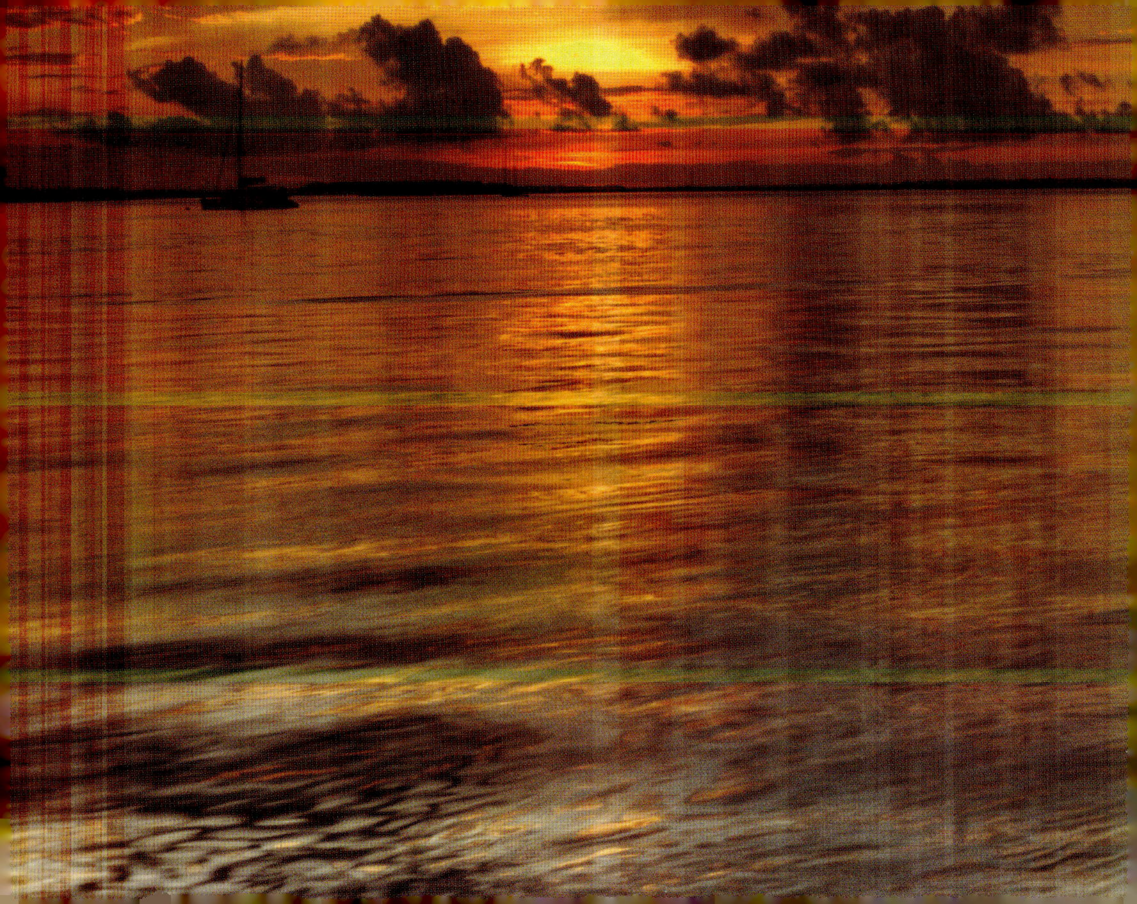

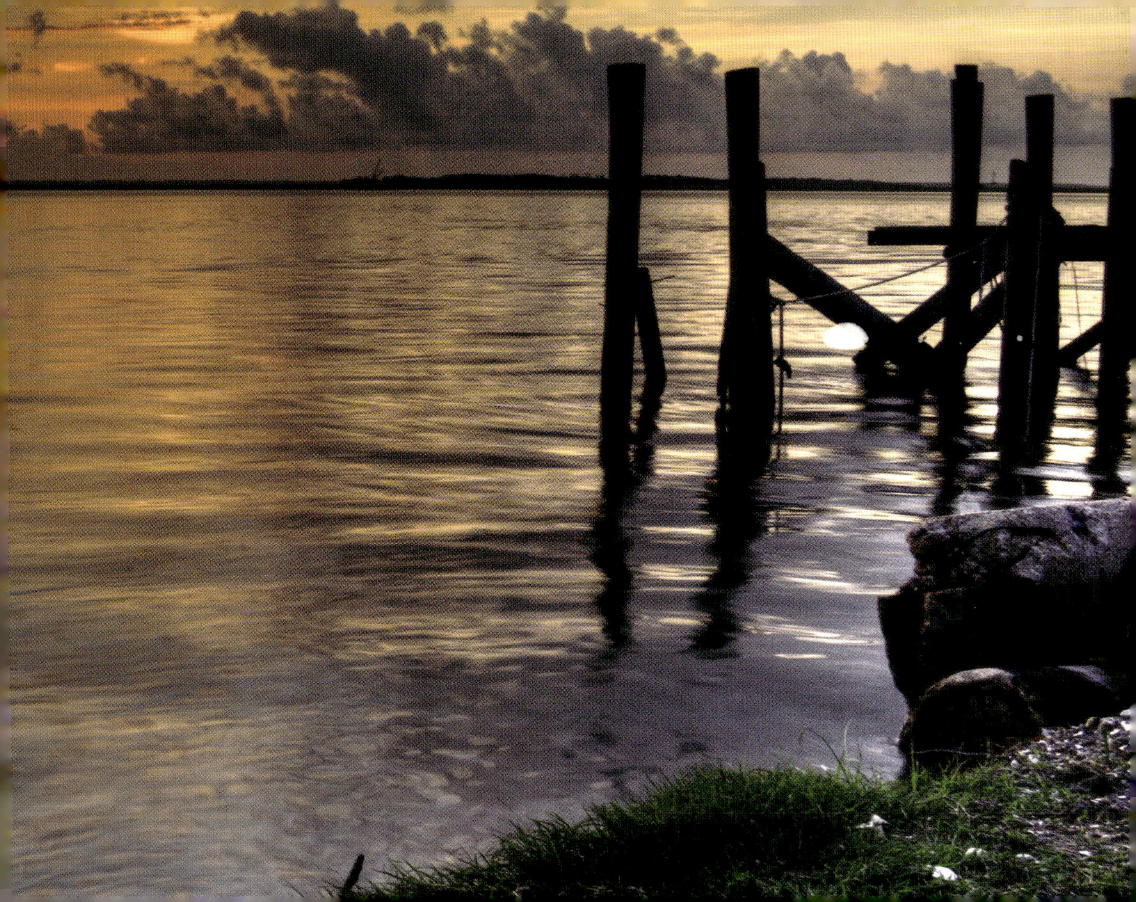

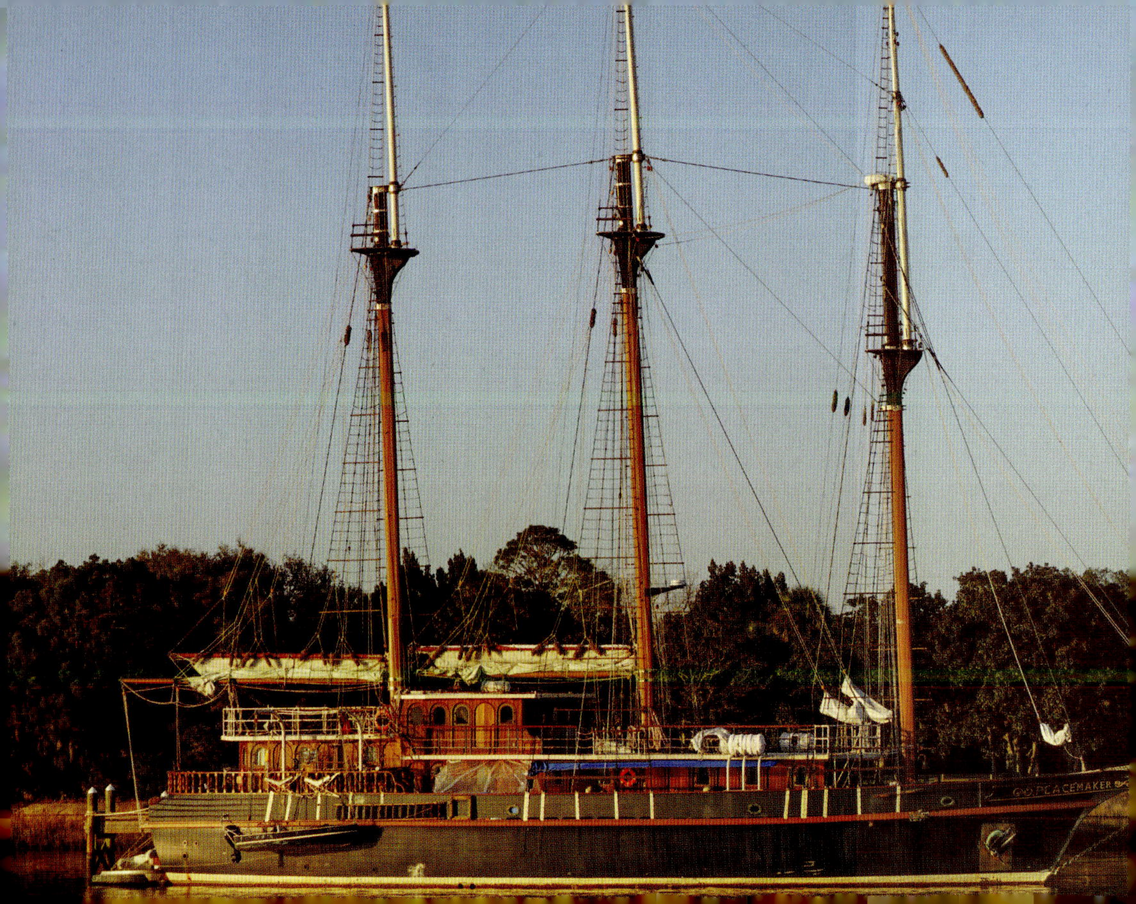
PEACEMAKER

PREVIOUS PAGES:
St Marys River, Amelia Island
The 200km (126 mile) river rises in the Okefenokee swamp and forms part of the border between Florida and Georgia.

OPPOSITE:
Peacemaker
Docked at St Mary's on Amelia Island, *Peacemaker* is an American barquentine and one of many yachts that call Florida home.

LEFT:
Amelia Island Lighthouse
Built in 1838, this lightouse is older than Florida state itself.

ABOVE AND RIGHT:

Boca Raton

First incorporated in 1924, Boca Raton (Spanish for 'mouse's mouth') is home to Florida Atlantic University and is one of the principal cities included in the Miami Metropolitan area. Architect Addison Mizner was the driving force behind the creation and incorporation of modern Boca Raton and the Mizner Park development is named after him. The original inlet named Boca Raton by Spanish colonists was further south, nearer Miami, and the name of the current city is the result of an old mapping mistake.

59

ALL PHOTOGRAPHS:
Hollywood, Florida
Hollywood started as one of the classic Atlantic Coast beach towns in 1925. Its white sand beaches have been joined by casinos (including the Hard Rock Casino pictured), golf courses, hotels (2,400 of them by 1960) and restaurants. One of the first of the 'planned communities' that proliferated during the Florida boom of this period, Hollywood was an early destination for 'snowbirds' (northerners who flee their cold winter weather and head to Florida). It has now grown into the twelfth-largest city in Florida, despite having suffered repeated hurricane damage over the years.

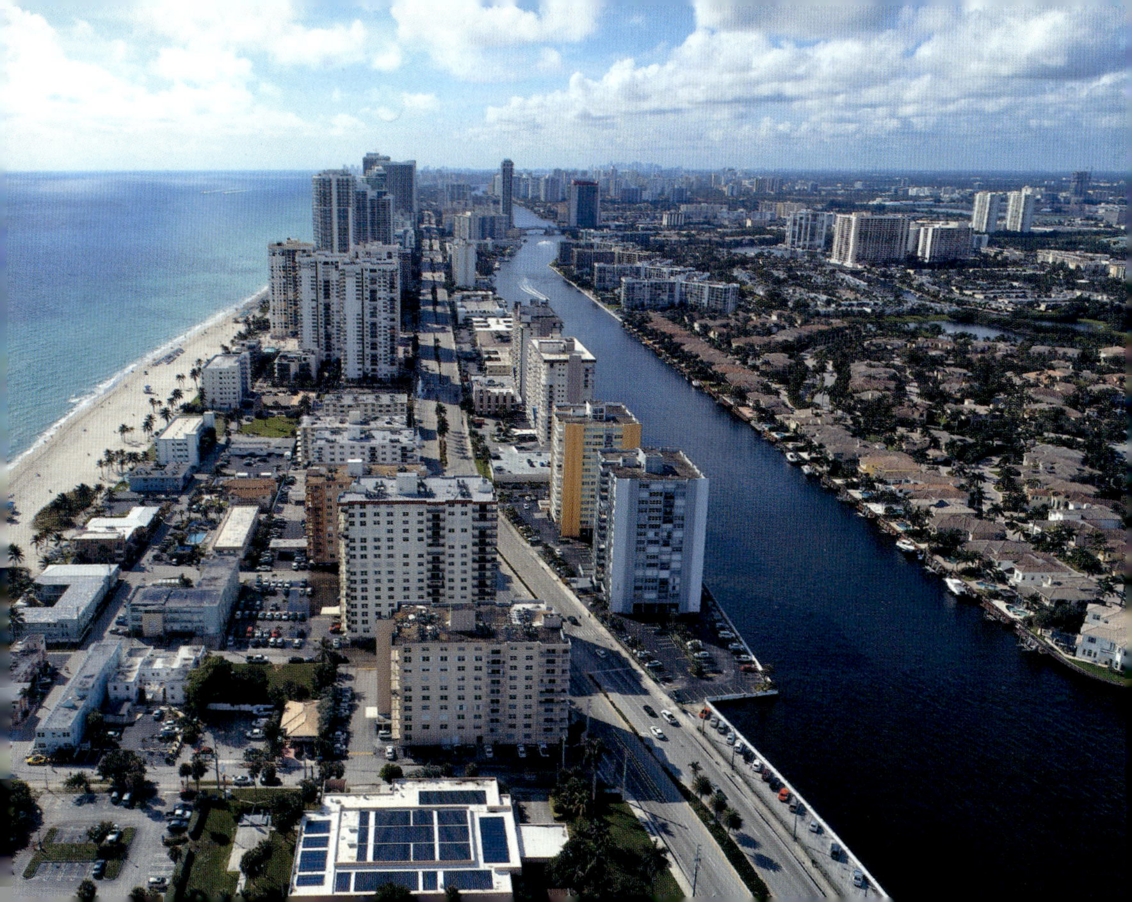

ALL PHOTOGRAPHS:
Kennedy Space Center, Cape Canaveral
One of 10 NASA launch sites, the Kennedy one is located on Merritt Island, which it shares with a state wildlife and bird sanctuary. Starting as a combination of the civilian Launch Operations Center and the military Cape Canaveral station it was named after the recently assassinated president, on 29 November 1963.

...the eyes of the world now look into space,
to the moon and to the planets beyond
and we have vowed that we shall not see
it governed by a hostile flag of conquest,
but by a banner of freedom and peace.
-John F. Kennedy

ALL PHOTOGRAPHS:
Kennedy Space Center, Cape Canaveral
It has been home to many space projects and programmes, including Skylab, Apollo, the Shuttle, and more. The Visitors Center is a popular tourist destination and the starting point for tours of the site. In 2019, a new statue was erected to celebrate the Apollo 11 astronauts Neil Armstrong, Buzz Aldrin and Michael Collins, the first men to walk on the Moon, in 1969.

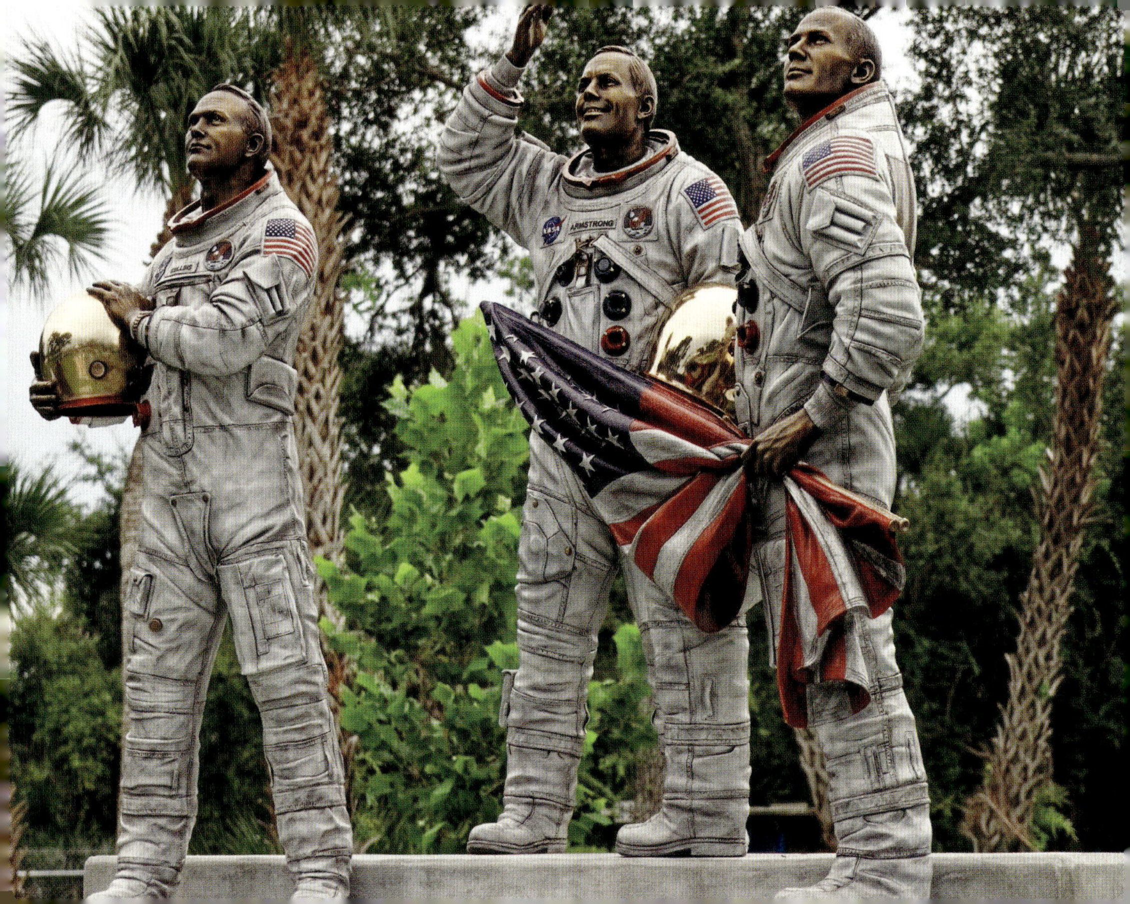
ARMSTRONG

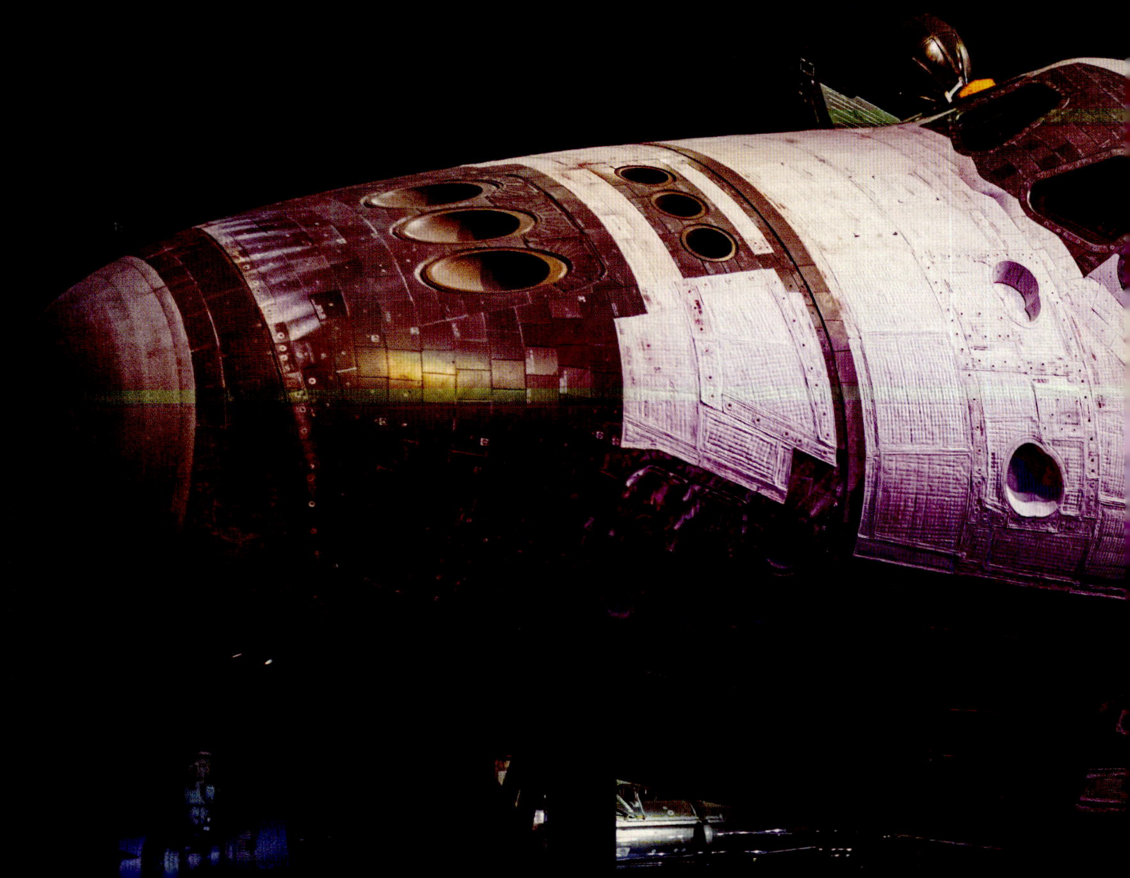

Shuttle Atlantis, Kennedy Space Center

The launch of the Shuttle, usually visible on its pad from the neighbouring nature reserve, always drew huge crowds that lined all the surrounding roads. Built in 1985, Atlantis flew the final shuttle mission of the program in 2011 and did 4,848 orbits of the earth, logging 203 million kilometres (126 million miles). It is now on display to the public.

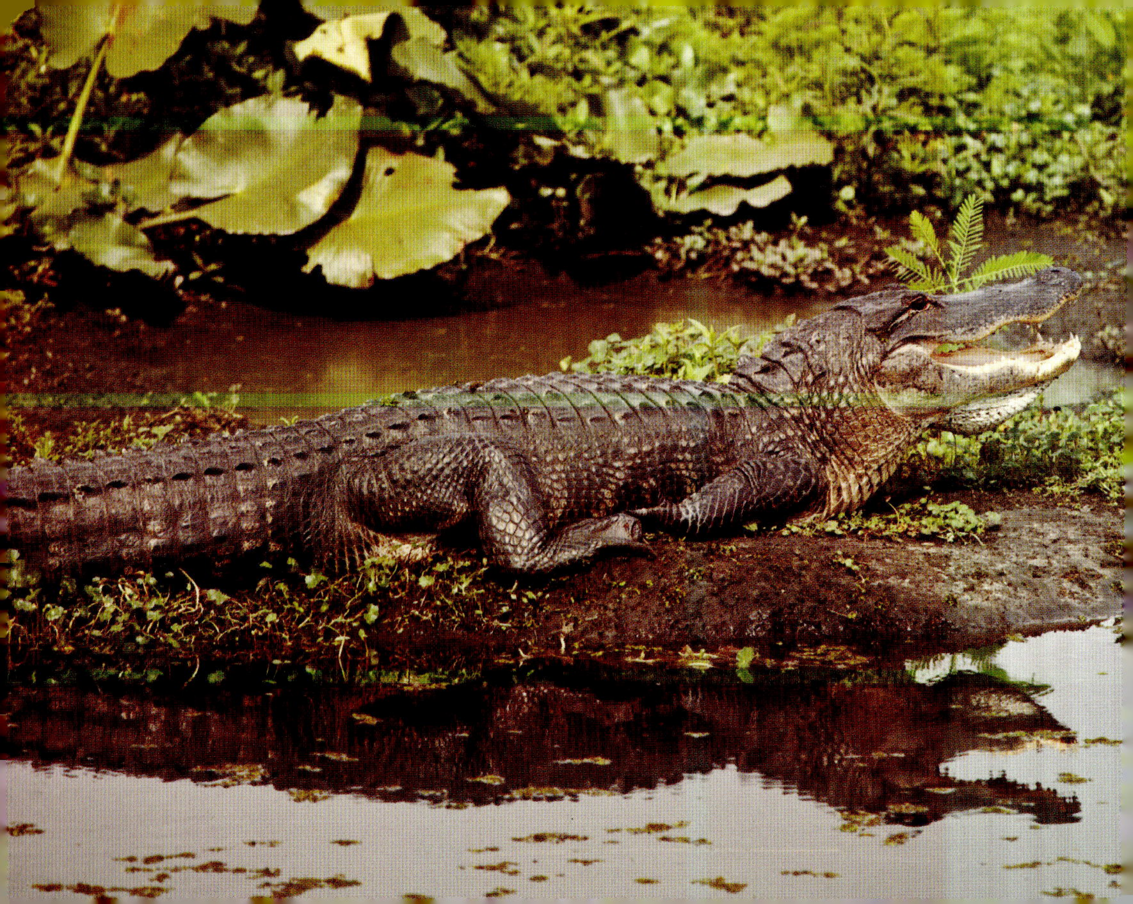

Panhandle and the West Coast

There is an old saying that the farther north you go in Florida the farther south you end up. This means that the people, culture, flora and fauna, and even the accents in the Panhandle are closer to those of Georgia and Alabama than they are to south Florida and Miami. White sand beaches and time warp small towns cater more to local and southern-state tourism than the northern and internationally focused south and east coast.

The west coast has Gulf of Mexico beaches and a different feel to the rest of the state, while still drawing many local Floridians and some northern tourism. Tampa Bay and Clearwater Beach, as well as some of the island resort communities, give the west coast great fishing, dining and beach holidays for visitors and residents alike. Like the rest of the state, it is vulnerable to the weather and has historically been lashed by violent hurricanes.

OPPOSITE:
Alligator
Alligators are common in Florida. These prehistoric reptiles are expert hunters in water and can run as fast as 7km/h (11mph) on dry land, even though it is uncommon for them to chase humans.

ALL PHOTOGRAPHS:
Destin

Destin is named after a Connecticut fishing boat captain who settled there in the mid-1800s. Well-known for its white sand beaches and emerald green water, it claims to have the biggest fishing fleet in the state and most people who visit come to charter a boat. Destin is on a panhandle peninsula that used to be a barrier island and that separates the Gulf of Mexico from Choctawhatchee Bay. The completion of the Choctawhatchee–West Bay Canal has technically made the peninsula an island again.

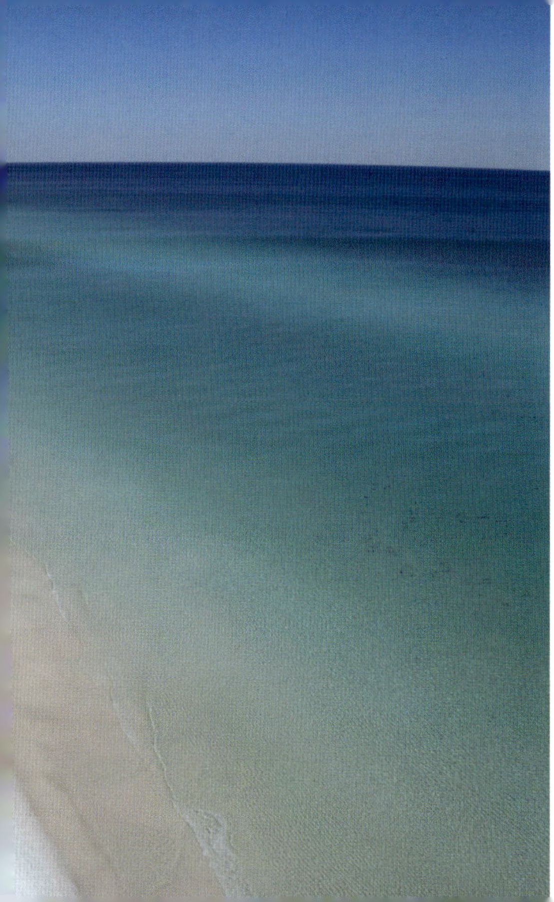
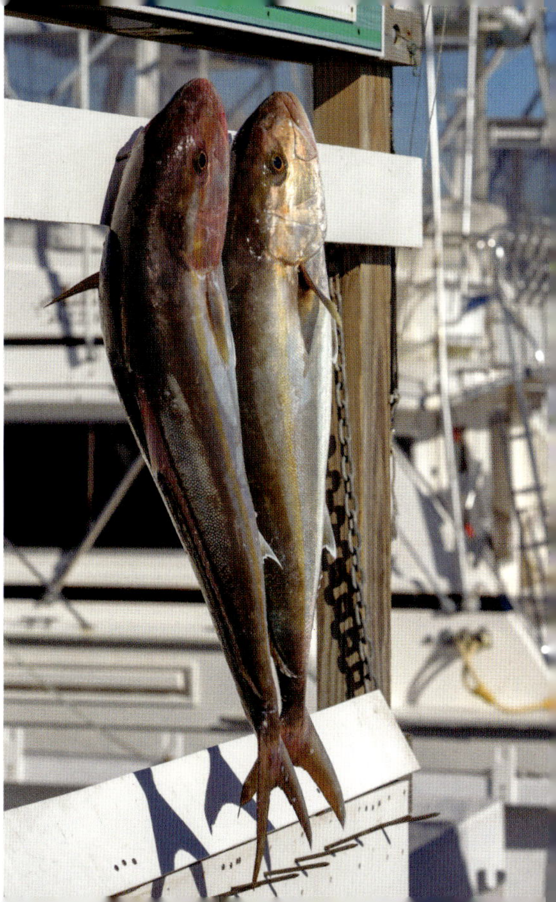

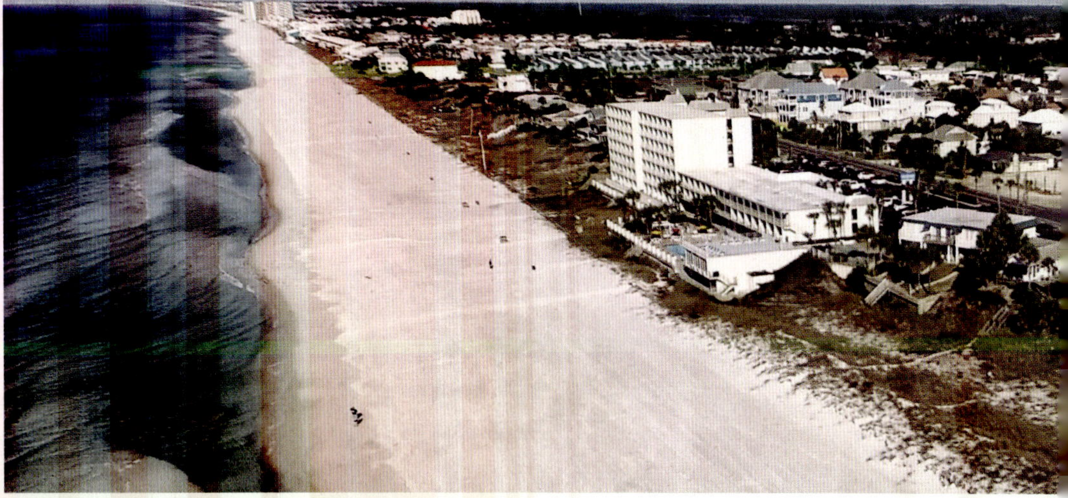
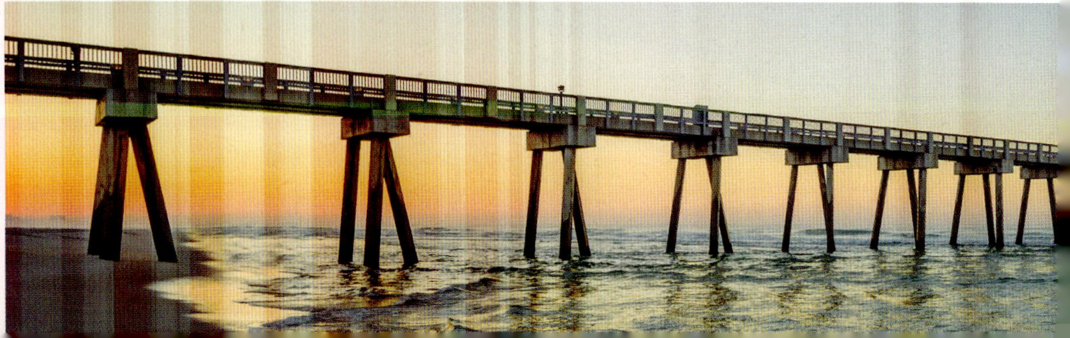

LEFT ABOVE:
Panama City Beach
With 42km (27 miles) of white sand beaches and dozens of hotels for every budget, this spot labels itself the 'Spring Break Capital of the World', which both attracts and repels visitors in equal measure.

LEFT BELOW:
MB Miller County Pier, Panama City Beach
This 457m (1,500ft) pier allows visitors to fish, dine and watch the sunset with views of the Gulf and the beach.

ABOVE:
Tallahassee swampland
Poor drainage and low levels outside the city result in literally dozens of these wetland ecosystems.

RIGHT:
Brokaw-McDougall House, Tallahassee
Built in 1860 by Peres Brokaw on land originally inhabited by the Appalachee Native Ameicans, then later the French, the McDougall name became attached when Brokaw's daughter married a Scotsman, Alexander McDougall. The house is a fine example of an antebellum, Classical Revival building with Italianate influences. The home was put on the National Register of Historic Places in 1972.

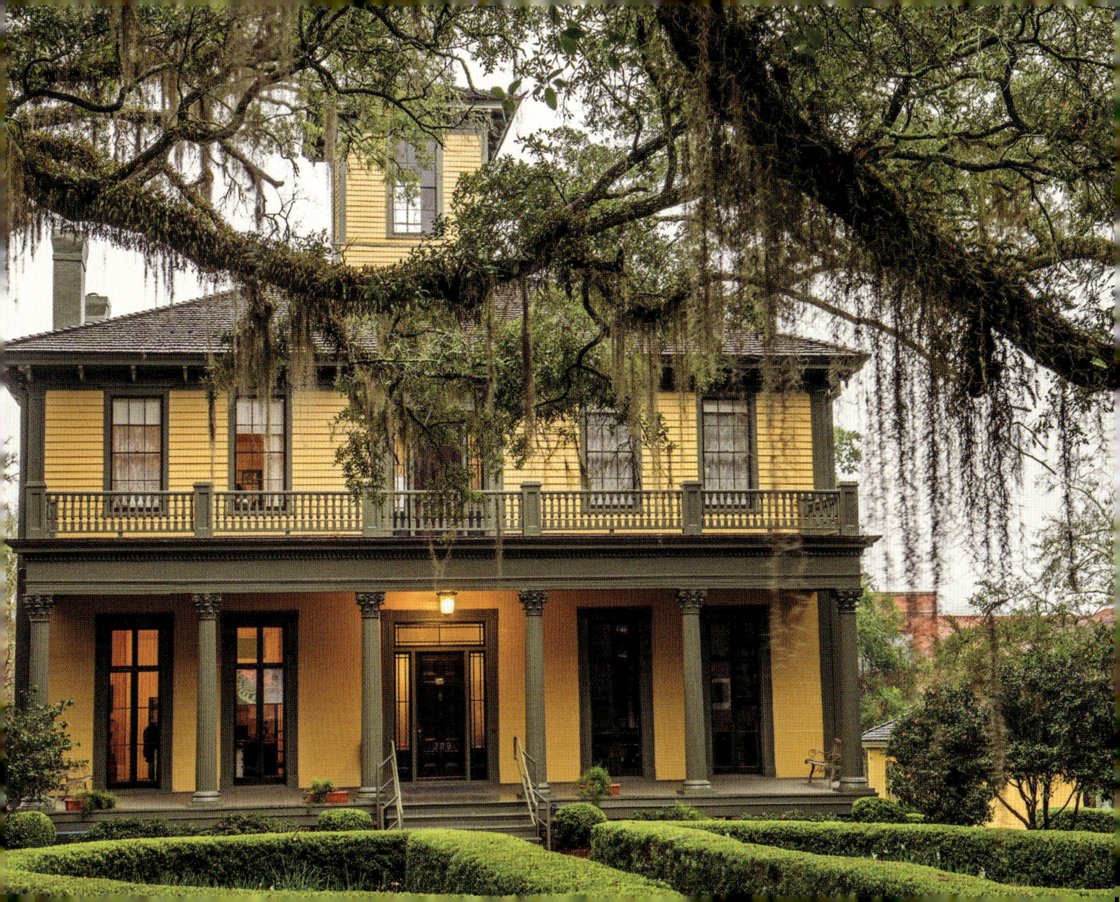

RIGHT:

Marching Chiefs, Doak Cambell Stadium, Tallahassee

The Marching Chiefs are the Florida State University band that entertains at Doak Campbell Stadium at The Seminoles' home games.

OPPOSITE:

Red Hills horse trials, Tallahassee

Red Hills serves as a qualifying event for riders looking for a place in national equestrian events, the Olympics and World Equestrian Trials. There is a long-standing social scene surrounding the industry and many people from Kentucky, the traditional home of the equine industry, have moved to Florida.

77

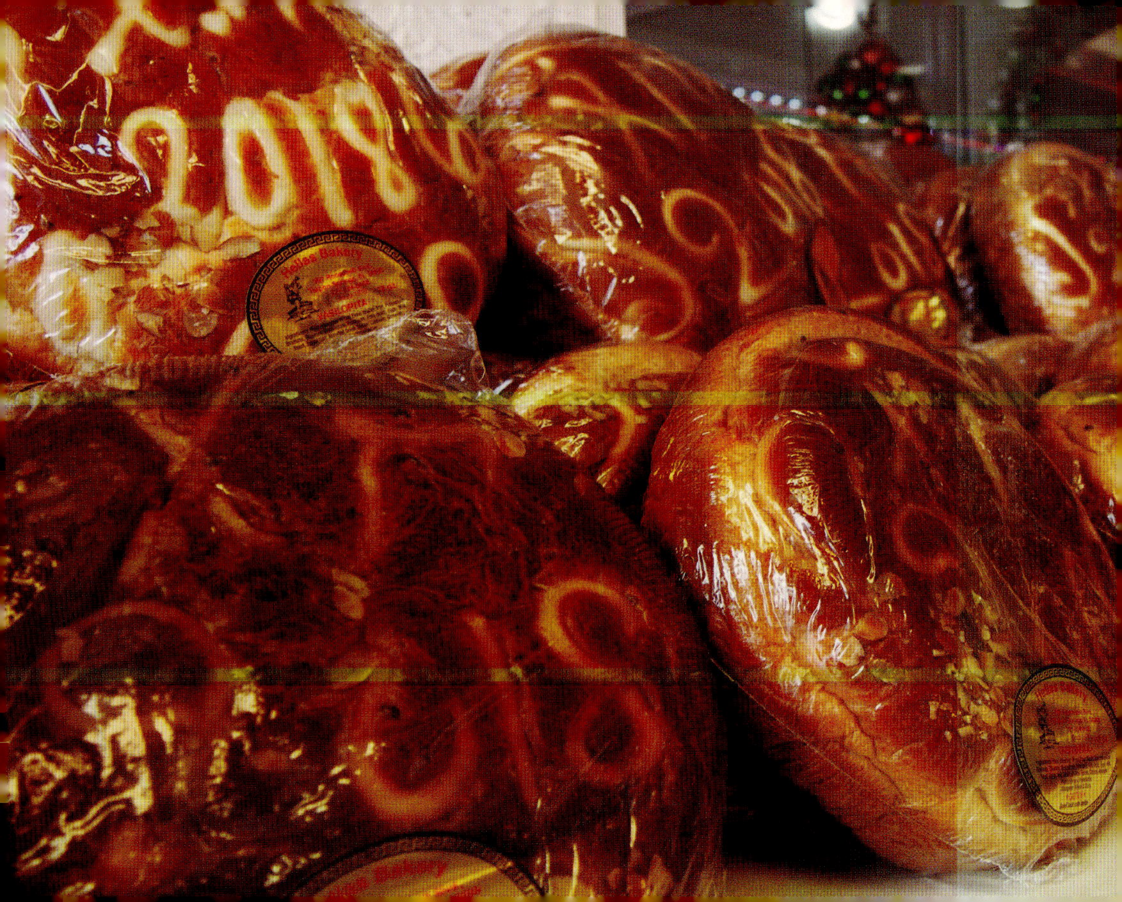
2018
Hellas Bakery

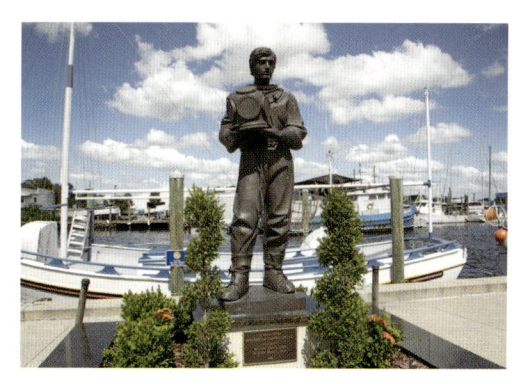

ALL PHOTOGRAPHS:
Tarpon Springs
Set in a corner of the Tampa Bay area, Tarpon Springs was founded by Greek settlers who developed it into Florida's once-thriving sponge fishing industry. One in ten residents still claims Greek heritage, and Greek restaurants and cultural references are ubiquitous. The sponge diver statue stands on the docks as a memorial to the city's past.

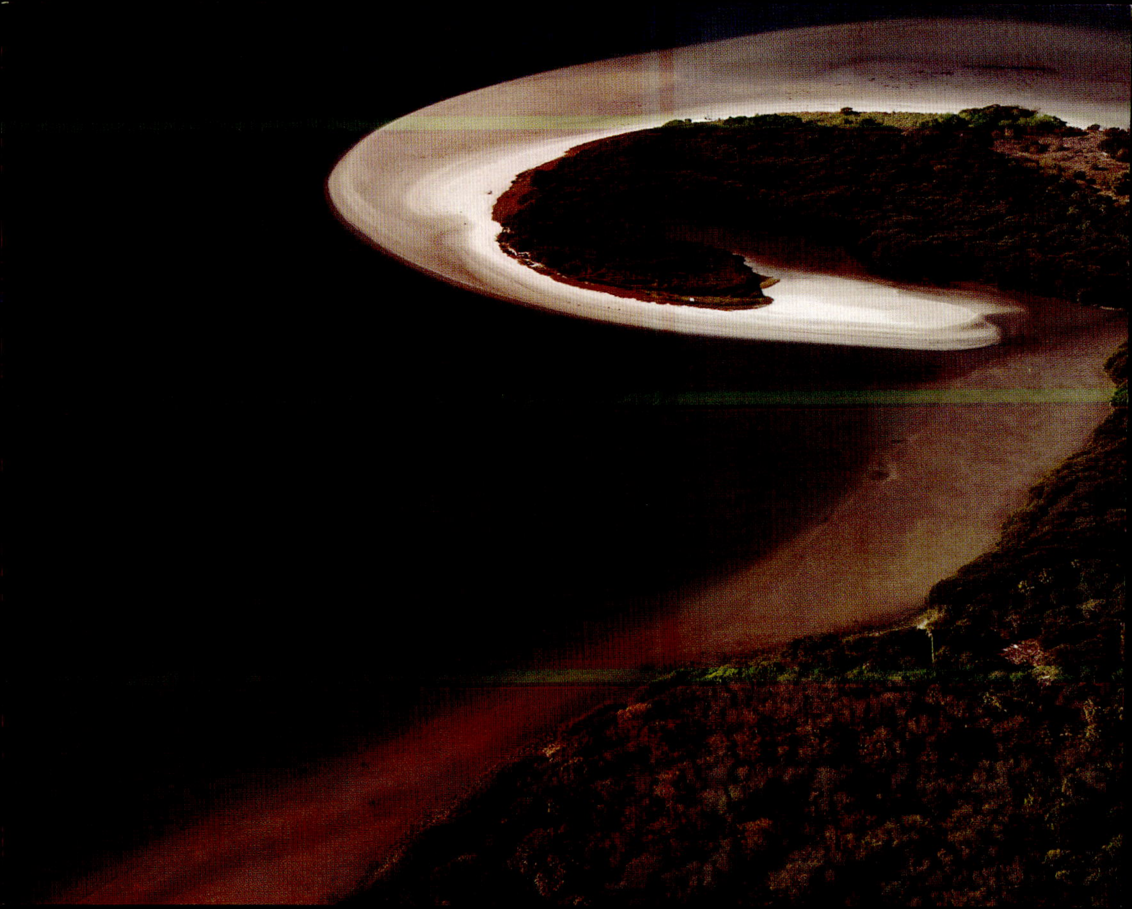

Tampa Bay
One of many sandbars off the coast of Tampa Bay. On the west coast, Tampa Bay is an estuary off the Gulf of Mexico that includes Lower Tampa Bay, Middle Tampa Bay, Old Tampa Bay, Hillsborough Bay and McKay Bay.

The arrival of the Spaniards in the 1500s resulted in the indigenous tribes being decimated by disease and conflict, and the area languished for a century until the United States took possession in 1821. The 20th century brought massive growth in both population and business and today the area is a major commercial and population hub.

Ray's
CAR
429
HECHO
CIGAR CITY
BREWING
Jai Alai
INDIA PALE ALE
CIGAR CITY
BREWING
429
PLEASE DRINK
RESPONSIBLY
CIGAR CITY
BREWING

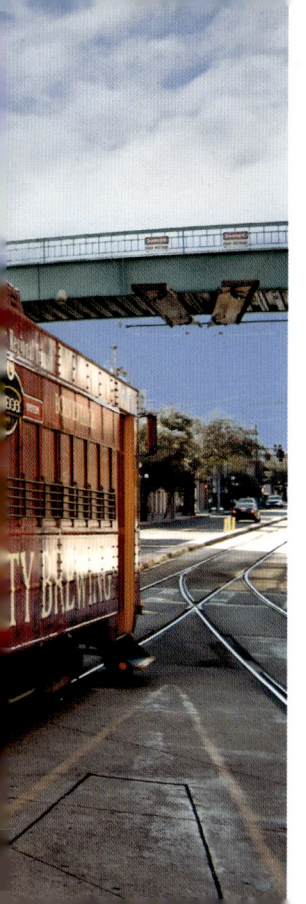

LEFT:

Tampa streetcar
Started in 1895, the Tampa streetcars made almost 26 million passenger journeys in 1926, but bus service and car ownership greatly reduced passenger numbers and the service ended after World War II. The previous 34km (21 miles) of track have been cut back to 4km (2.4 miles), carrying passengers between Ybor City, the Channel District, and the Convention Center.

ABOVE:

Tampa Skyline on Hillsborough River
The Hillsborough river, named for the British Secretary of State for the Colonies who controlled the pensions of the surveyors who named it, flows 97km (60 miles) and passes through Tampa as it drains into Tampa Bay.

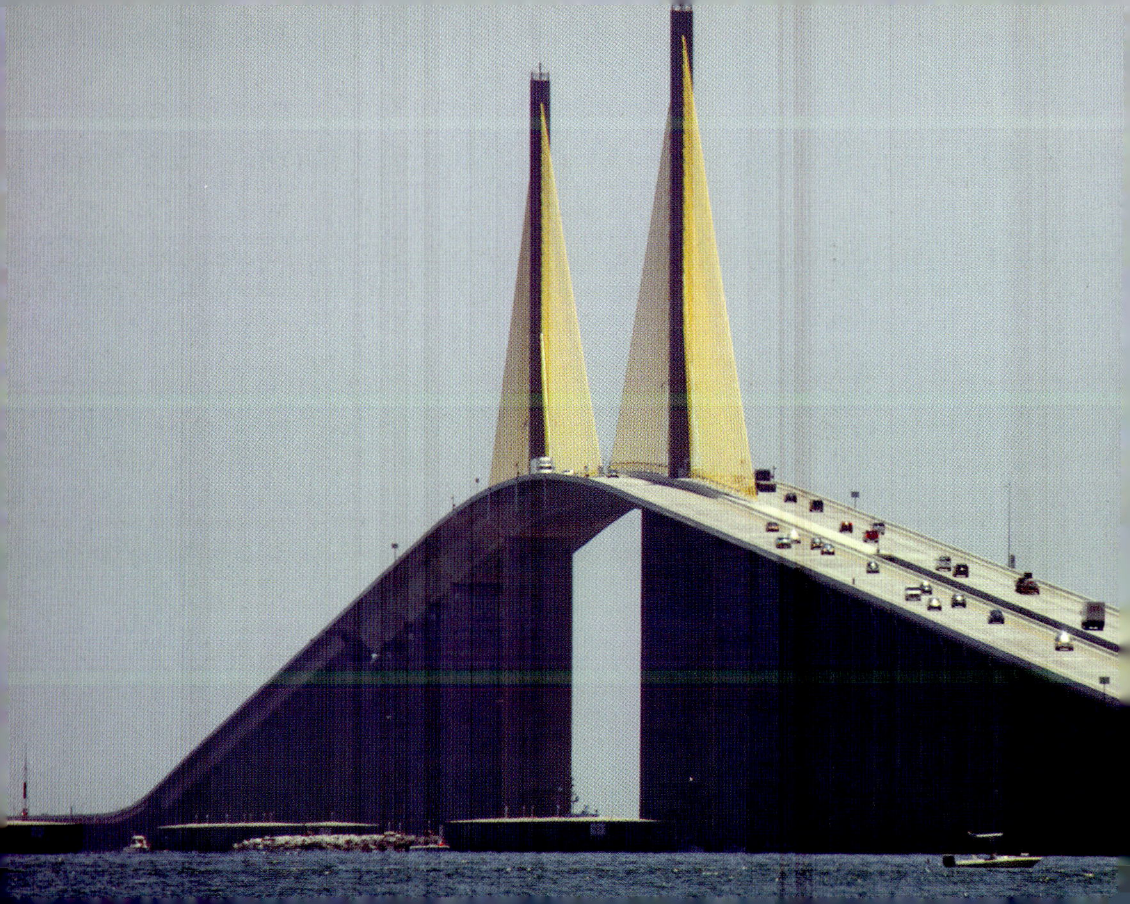

Sunshine Skyway Bridge, Tampa Bay

The Bob Graham Sunshine Skyway Bridge over lower Tampa Bay connects St Petersburg with Terra Ceia. The bridge was first built in 1954 before a collision with its supports in 1980 caused part of the span to collapse. The bridge was replaced in 1987 and part of the original converted into a fishing pier.

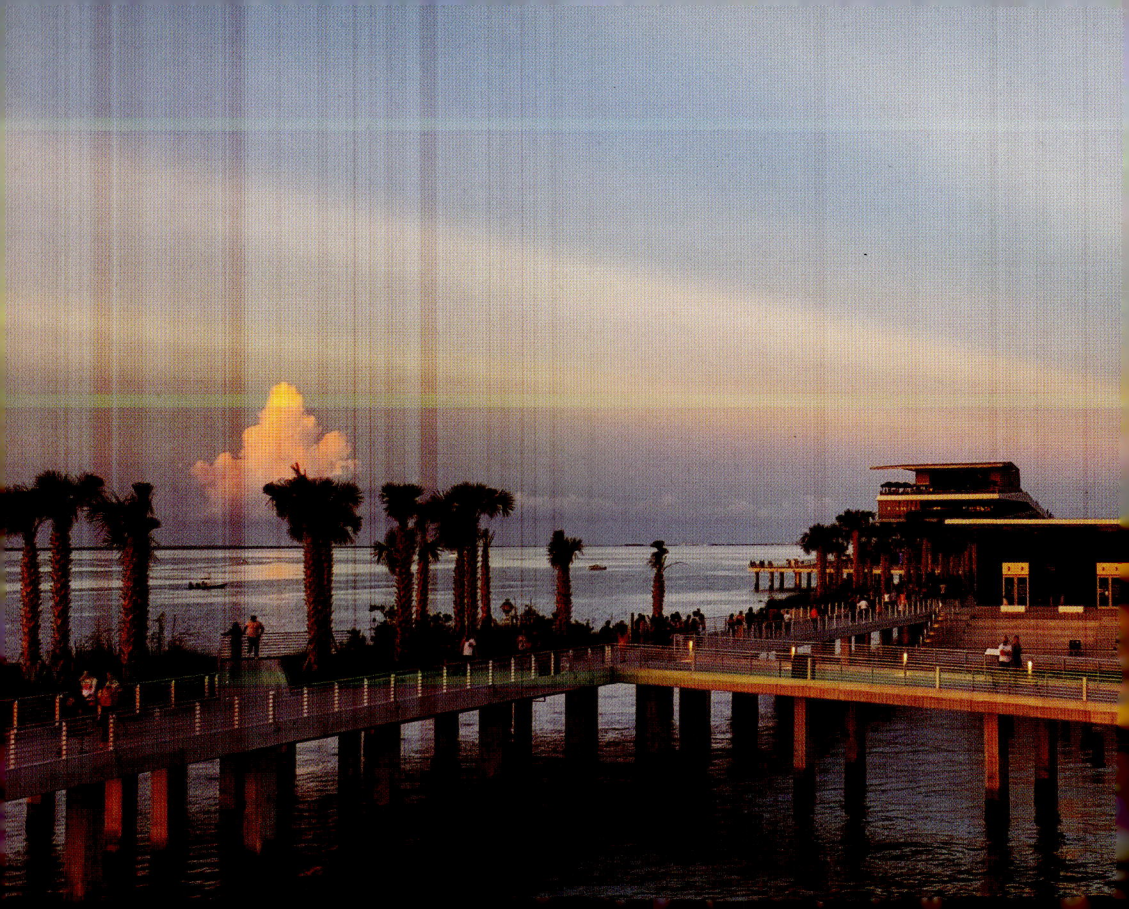

LEFT:
St Petersburg Pier
The pier is the showpiece of the district of the same name that features bars, restaurants, cafes, art exhibitions and a marina. Previous piers were built in 1889, 1896, 1906, 1913 and 1926.

OVERLEAF:
South Yacht basin, St Petersburg
This municipal marina serves the busy private boating scene around St Petersburg.

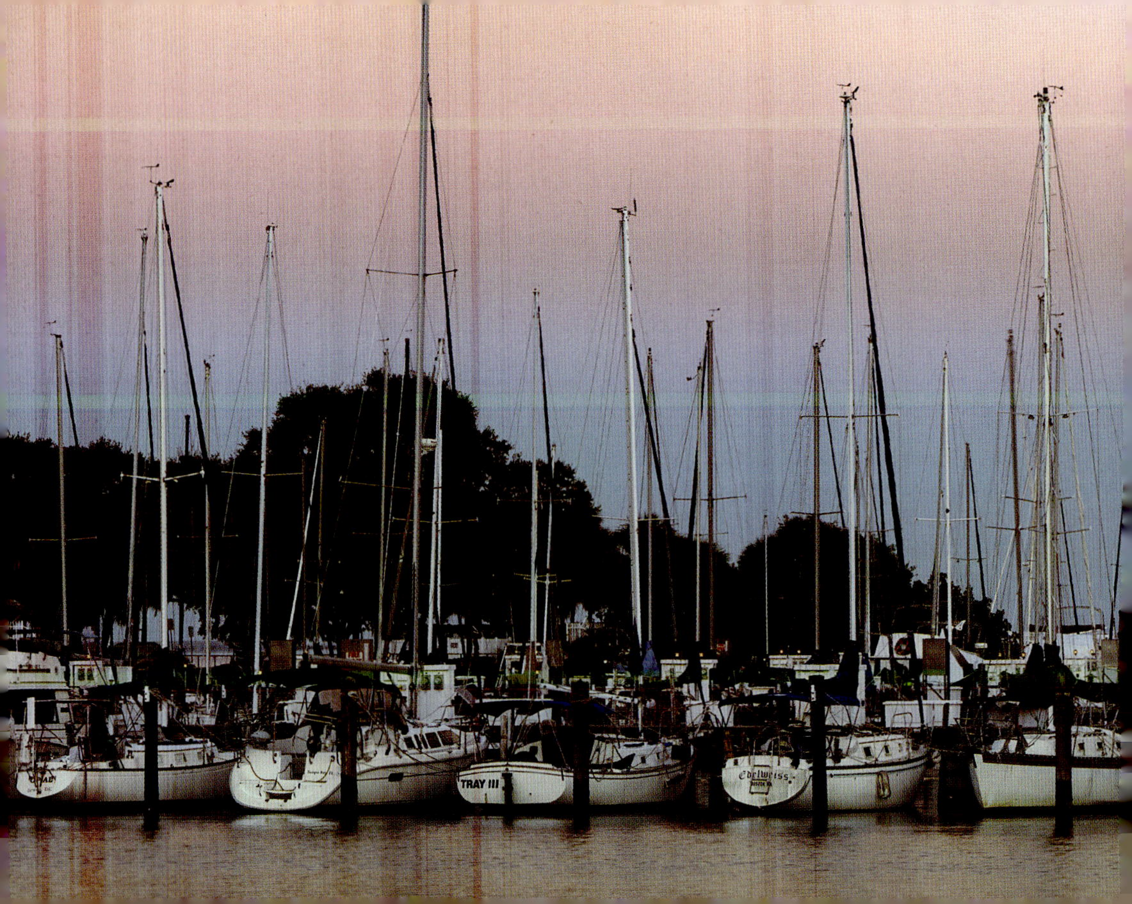
TRAY III
Edelweiss

FIRE HOSE
DESPERADO
Sea Angel
St. Petersburg
Florida
ANNA MARIE

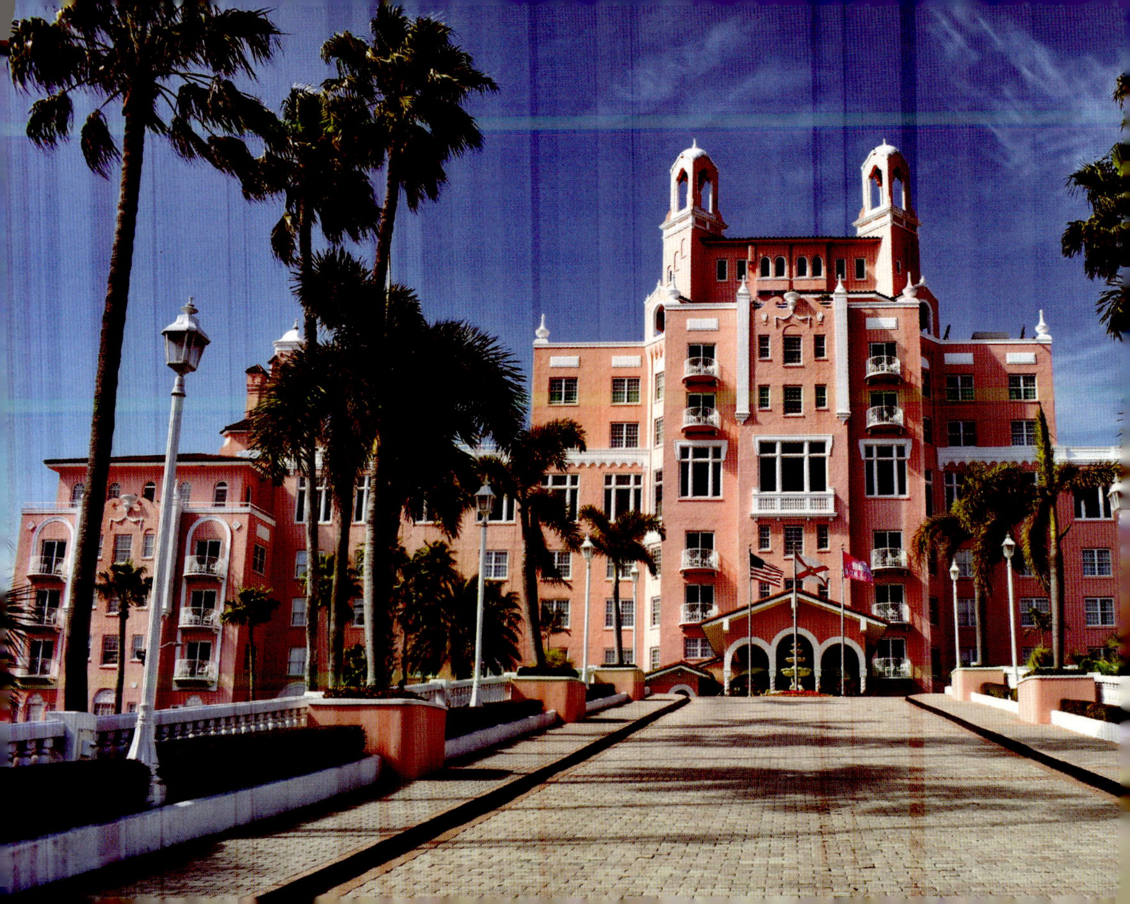

OPPOSITE:
Don Cesar Hotel, St Petersburg Beach
Having had multiple renovations since its opening in 1928 the hotel is a luxury spa that has hosted F. Scott Fitzgerald and other famous luminaries.

ABOVE AND BELOW LEFT:
Tropican Field, St Petersburg
This domed stadium was home to the Tampa Bay Rays and was previously home to the Tampa Bay Lightning, both Major League Baseball Teams. Originally known as The Thunderdome, it has hosted Davis Cup tennis, as well as many large rock concerts.

ALL PHOTOGRAPHS:
Hollis Gardens
Lakeland is a city that lies just over halfway between the Orlando and Tampa areas. It was settled by Europeans in the late 19th century who farmed cattle and grew citrus fruit, and mined phosphates. In it is Hollis Gardens, a formal botanical display garden that features neo-classical architecture, native trees and plants, and 10,000 flowers.

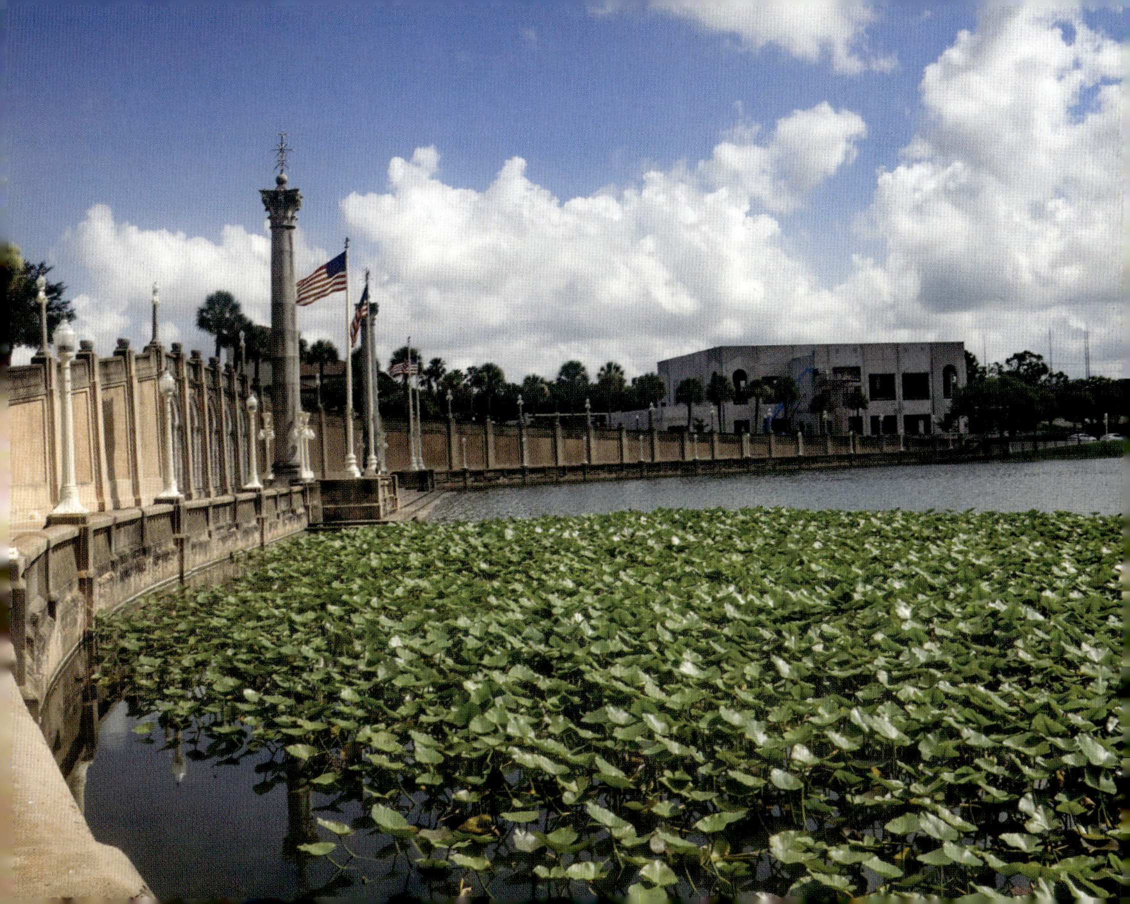

TROPICAL BUFFET
&
FREE
BEER, WINE & RUM PUNCH
CALYPSO BREEZE
NOW CRUISING
727-461-3113
WWW.CTCRUISES.COM

ALL PHOTOGRAPHS:
Madeira Beach
Known for fishing and dolphin-watching, as well as nesting sea turtles and beautiful beaches, Madeira has a healthy boating industry featuring vivid boats and brightly painted local restaurants and cafes. Its lovely white sand beaches and blue water attract international visitors, as well as local Floridians.

ALL PHOTOGRAPHS:
Sarasota
South of Tampa Bay, Sarasota was first seen on Spanish maps in 1763, before being settled by the Scottish in the mid-1800s after being bought for development by a Scottish insurance company. One landmark is a statue based on the famous *New York Times* photo of a sailor kissing a woman in Times Square, called 'Unconditional Surrender'. The Ca' d'Zan (opposite) is the Mediterranean revival-style residence of art collector John Ringling.

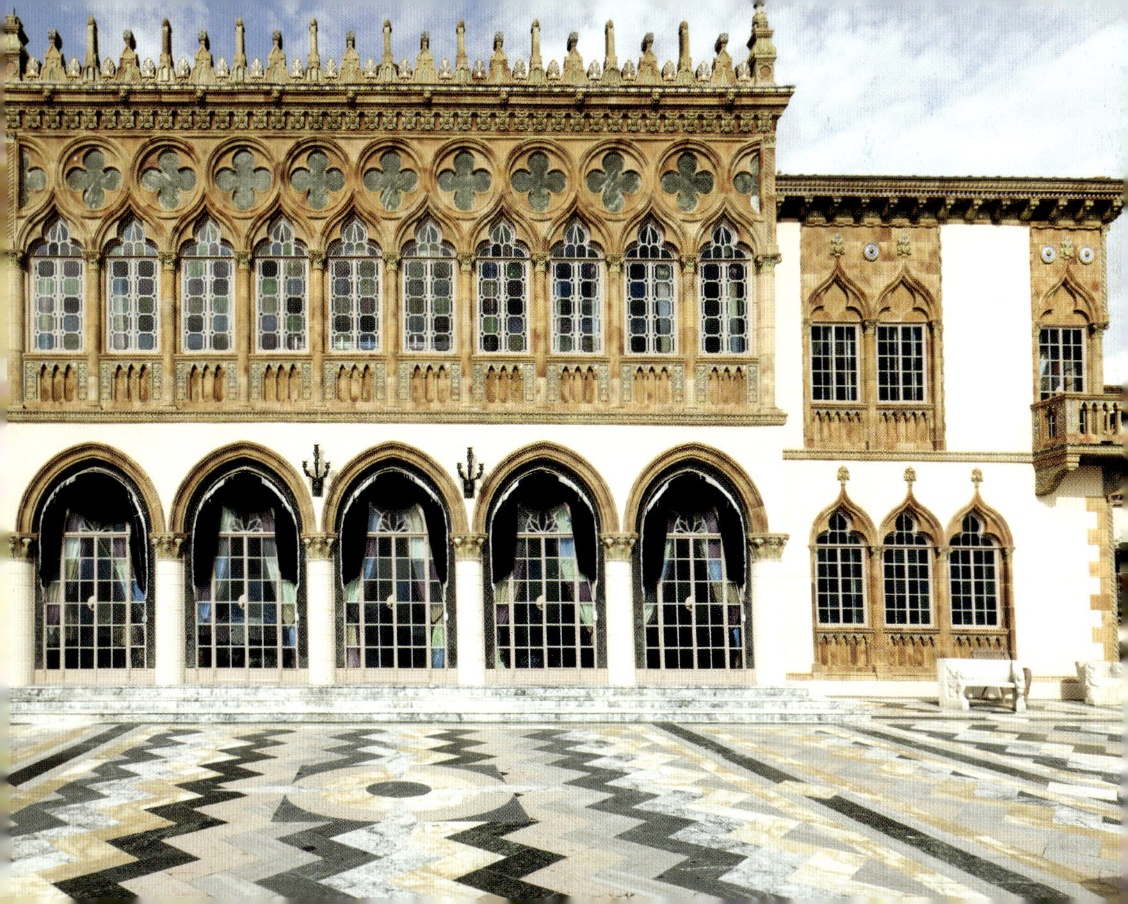

Ringling Museum, Sarasota

The John and Mabel Ringling Museum is the official art museum of the State of Florida and is known for its collection of paintings by Peter Paul Rubens, Velasquez and Van Dyck, as well as a circus museum. Originally put together by John Ringling, the circus impresario of the early 20th century and his wife, it features the acquisitions that Ringling brought back from all over the world, much of it Baroque. The building itself is a pink Renaissance-style palace with 21 separate galleries and many sculptures.

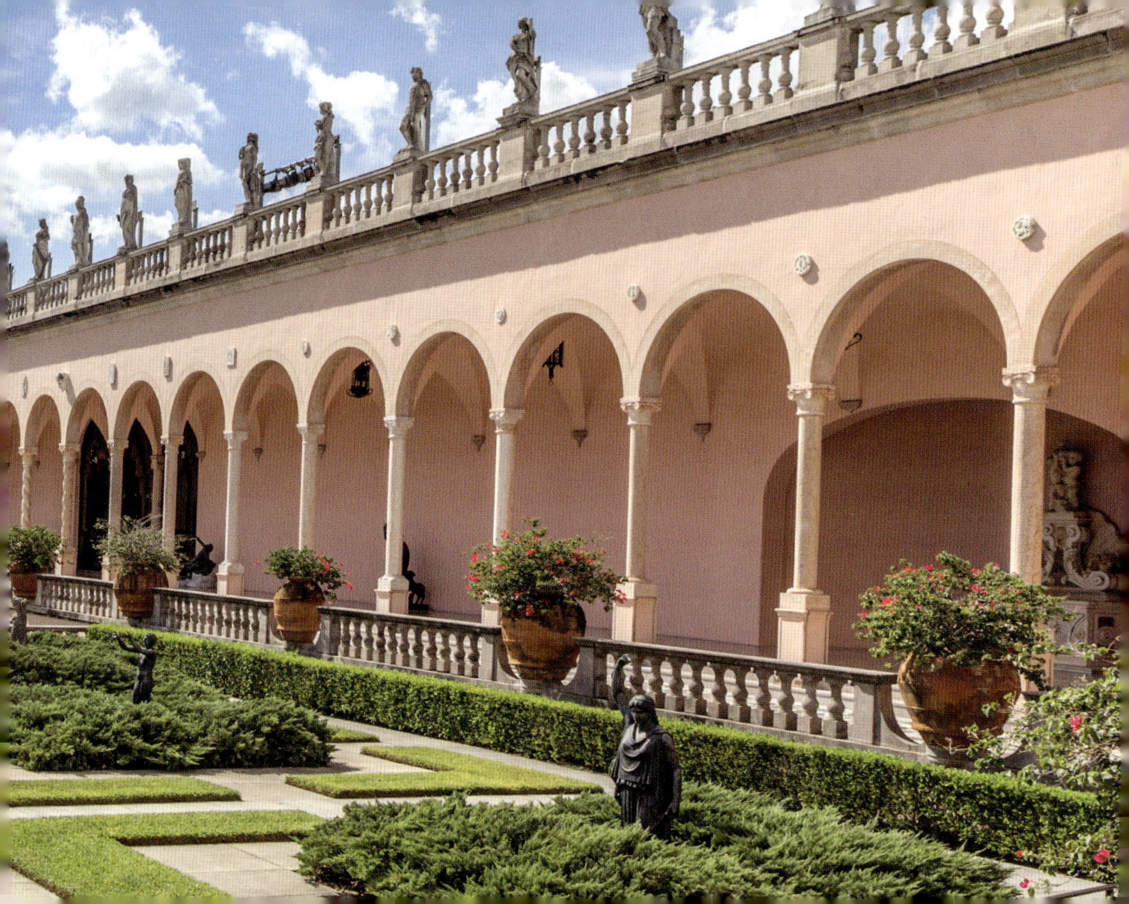

ALL PHOTOGRAPHS:
Fort Myers Beach
Located on Estero Island on the Gulf of Mexico the beach draws locals, snowbirds and regular tourists. Originally occupied by Calusa Native Americans, who were eventually decimated by European colonists, Cuban fishermen also worked here during the early 19th century, before the Homestead act of 1862 resulted in the arrival of American settlers.

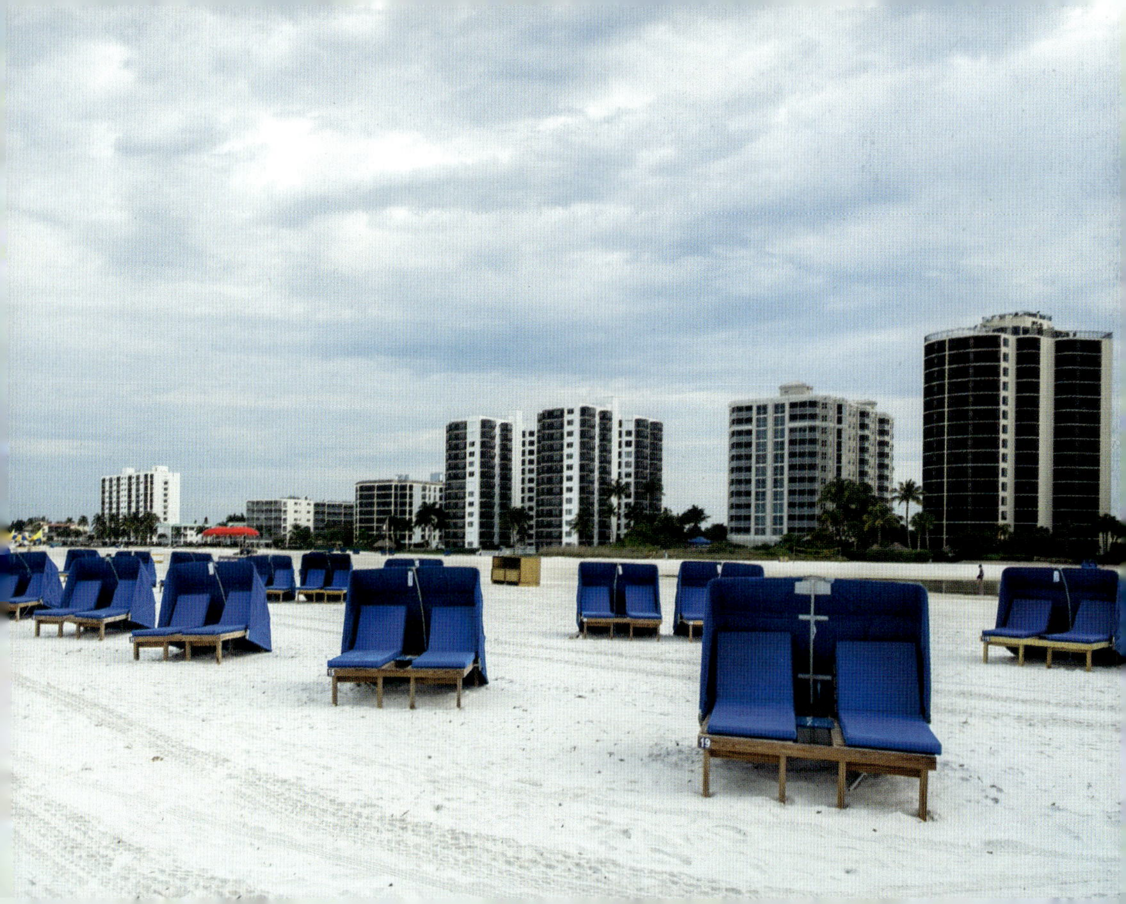

ALL PHOTOGRAPHS:
Naples
Naples was founded in 1886 and was another home of the Calusa Native Americans before European colonists decimated them. Its name came from promoters comparing its bay to the Bay of Naples in Italy, due to their similar climates and abundance of seafood. The railroad reached Naples in 1927 and the Tamiami Trail connected it to Miami the next year, but the anticipated surge of development didn't really kick in until the 1950s. Proximity to the Everglades brings ecotourists, as well as those looking for beaches and seaside entertainment.

103

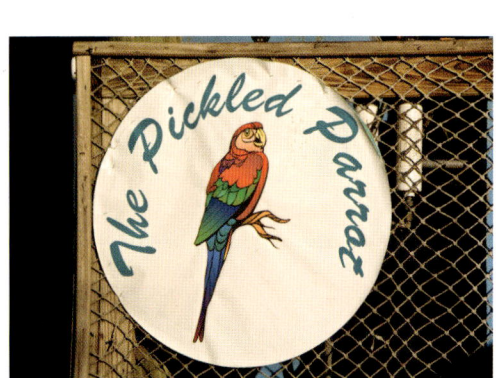

RIGHT:

Pitcher plants, Apalachicola National Forest

This forest is home to some of the most unique flora and fauna in the world, including the carnivorous pitcher plant, which catches and eats small insects. The plant is named after the goblet shape formed by its leaves.

OPPOSITE:

Barking tree frog, Apalachicola National Forest

Found in Florida and other east coast locations, this frog really does bark, as a mating call. It's the largest native tree frog in the US.

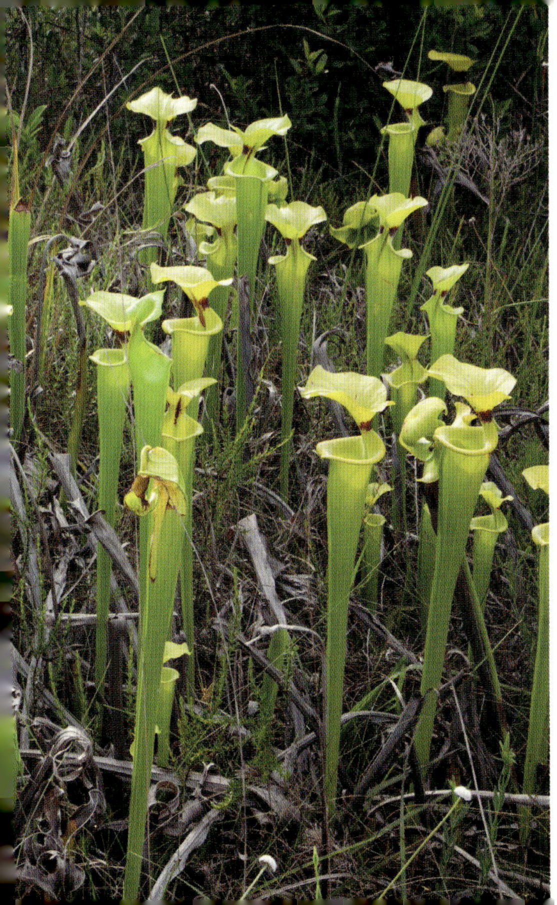
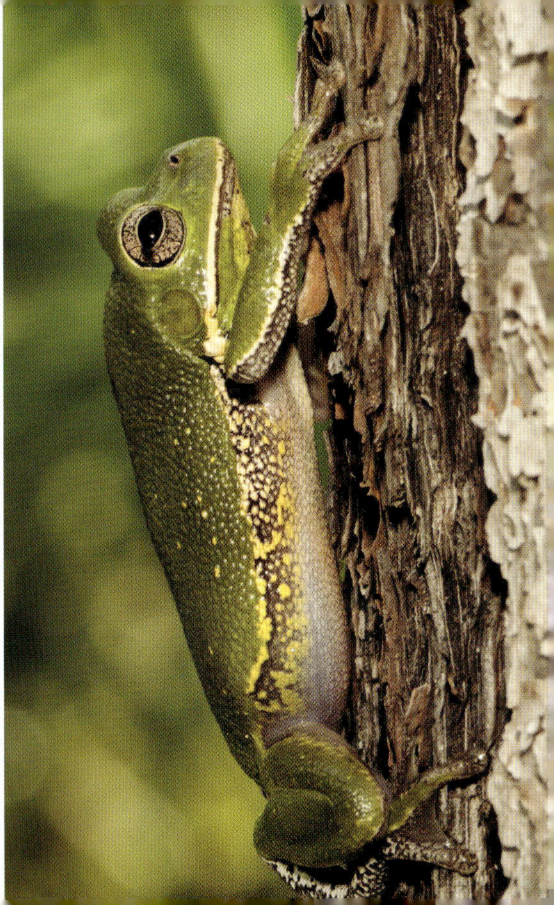

Ford's GARAGE
PRIME BURGERS | CRAFT BEER

LEFT:
Ford's Garage, Cape Coral
Ford's Garage won't fix your car but they will serve you a prime burger of a craft beer. There are branches scattered throughout central and southern Florida.

OVERLEAF:
White pelicans, Cedar Key
White pelicans are some of the largest birds in North America and with a 2.7m (9ft) wingspan far outstrip their brown cousins. Following years of declining population they have been coming back since the 1970s.

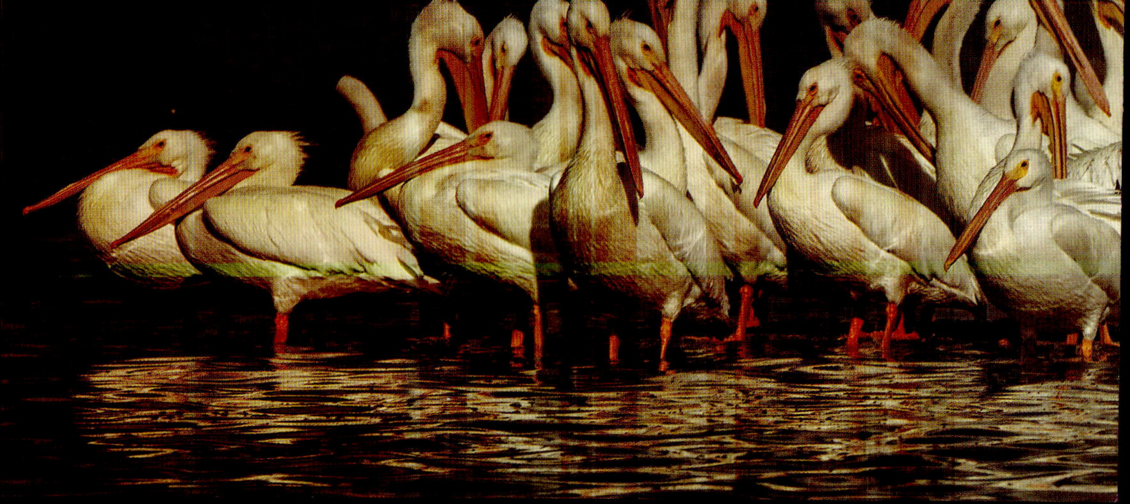

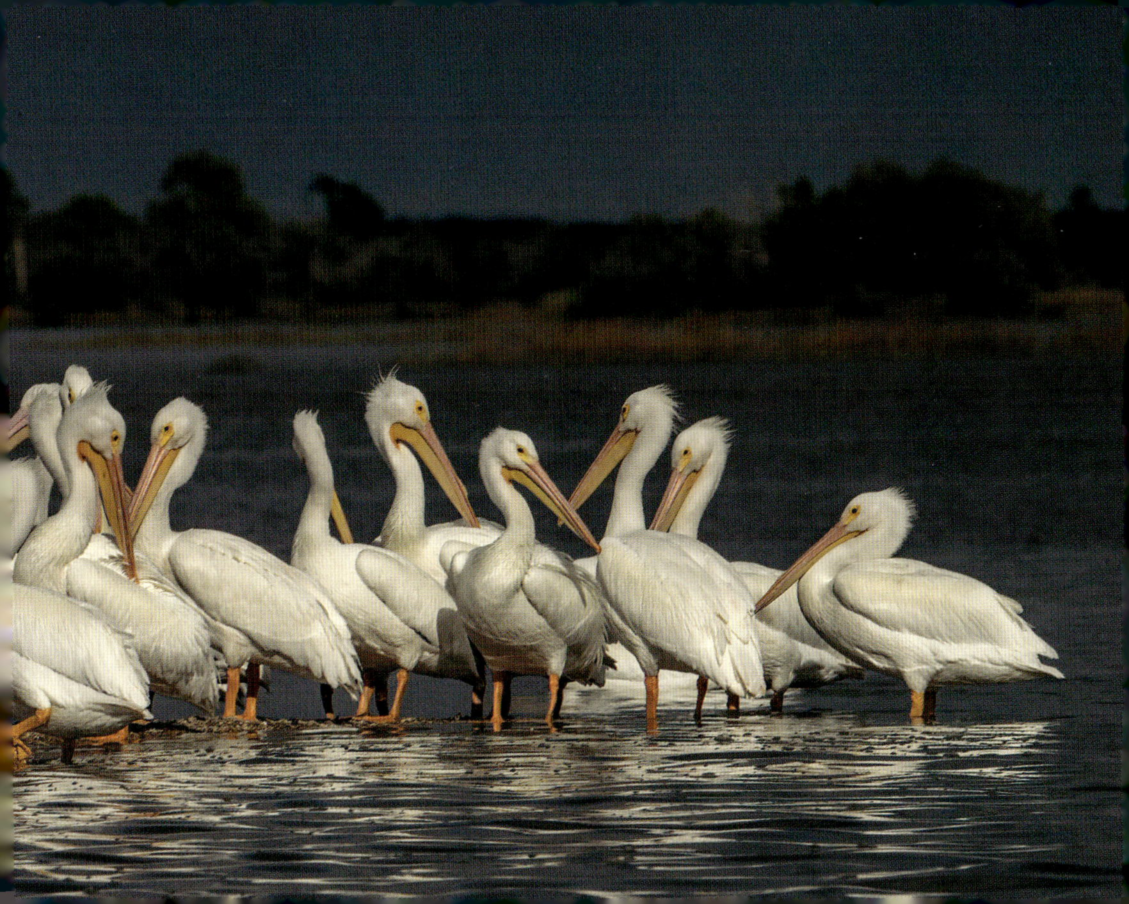

Cedar Key
A 1542 Spanish map called the area *Las islas de Sabine* – the Cedar Islands – named after the trees that used to grow there. The city of Cedar Key is on Way Key, 6km (4 miles) out in the Gulf of Mexico. The area is one of the largest producers of clams and oysters. It is also part of a National Wildlife Refuge and is home to bald eagles and roseate spoonbills. It is also known as an artists' colony, and the annual Fine Arts Festival is held the last weekend of March.

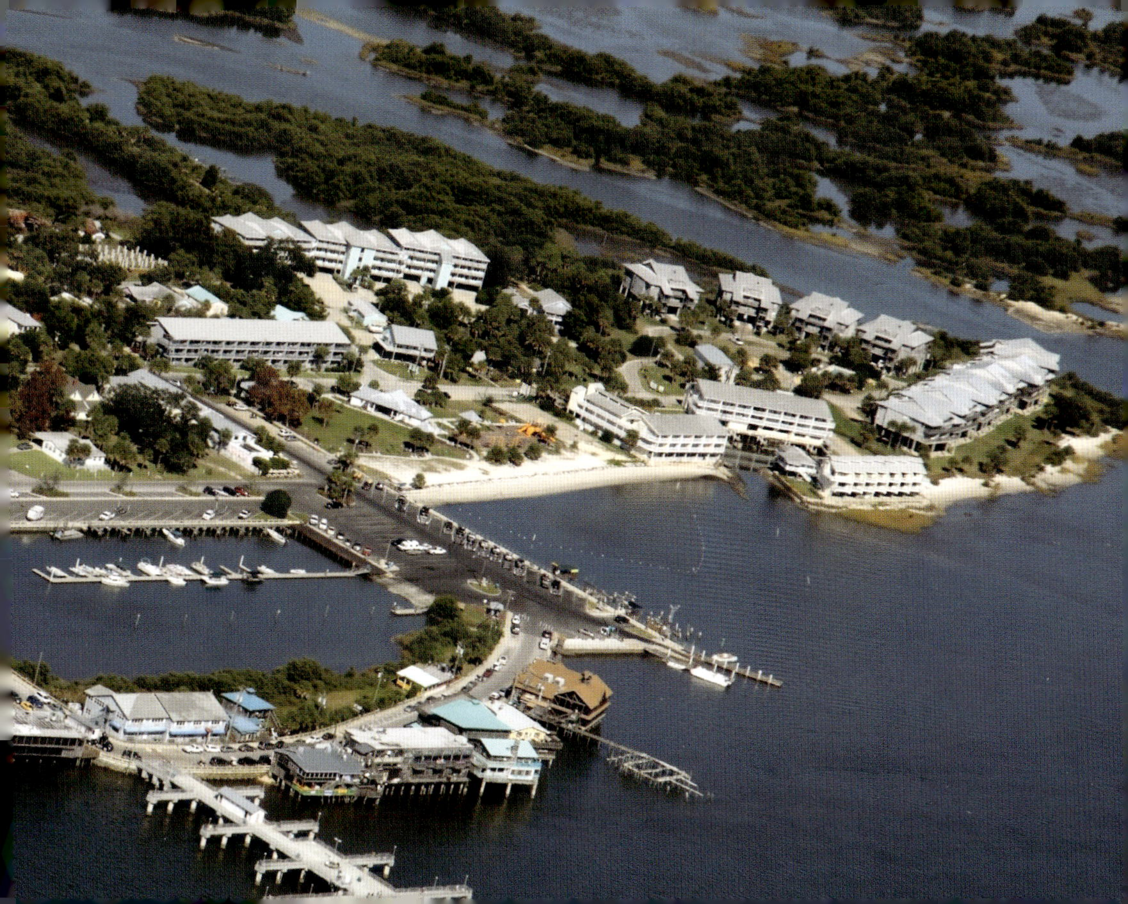

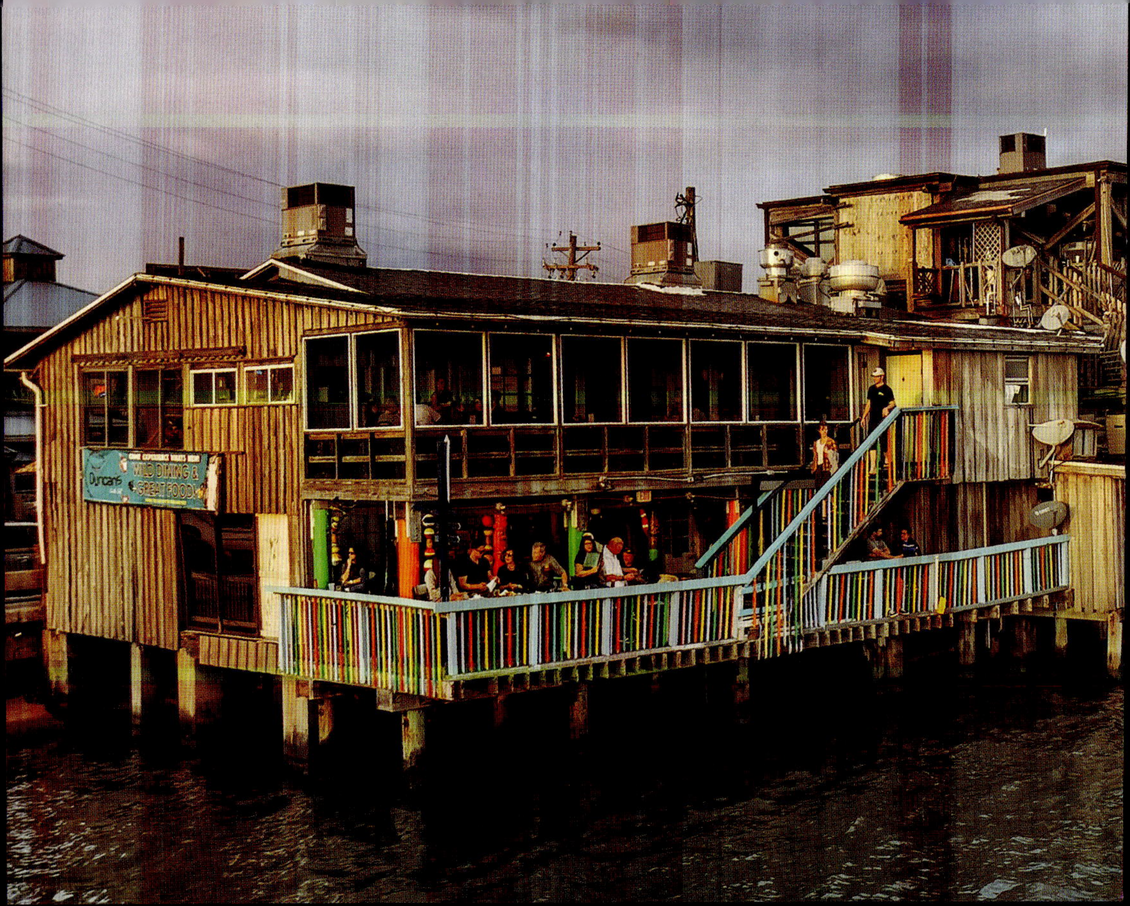
Duncans
WILD DINING &
GREAT FOOD

ALL PHOTOGRAPHS:
Waterfront, Cedar Key
Known as 'The Dock' to residents, the old waterfront is built on stilts and is constructed of old weathered wood. It features many shops and restaurants. Pelicans can be seen perching on poles, which reflects the area's status as a wildlife refuge.

ALL PHOTOGRAPHS THIS PAGE:
Paynes Prairie Ecopassage Nature State Park Preserve, Gainesville
Now designated a National Natural Landmark, this unique savannah is home to alligators, bison and 270 species of birds among the 420 vertebrates identified in natural habitats. The reserve is a jewel of Central Florida.

OPPOSITE:
Clearwater Beach
One of the best-known of the Gulf beaches and very convenient for those in the Tampa Bay area, it can be very crowded in season.

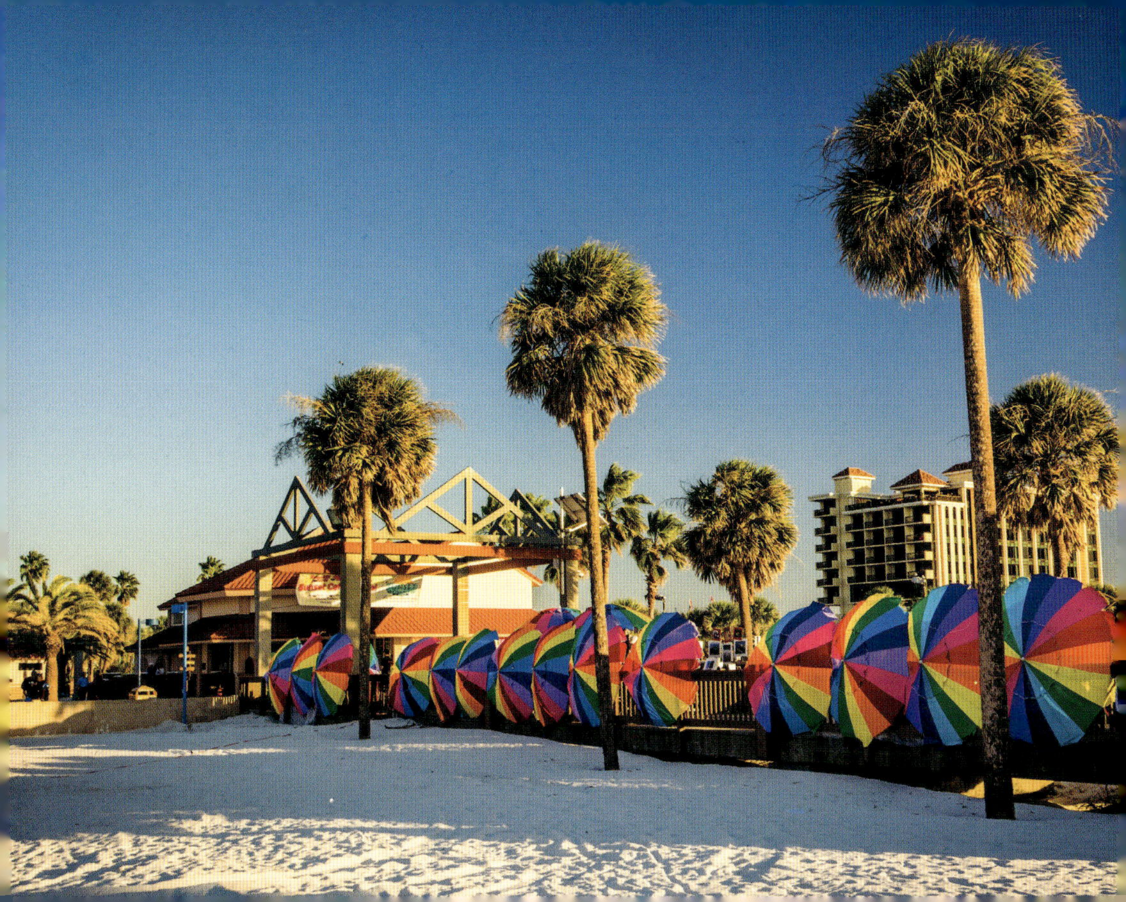

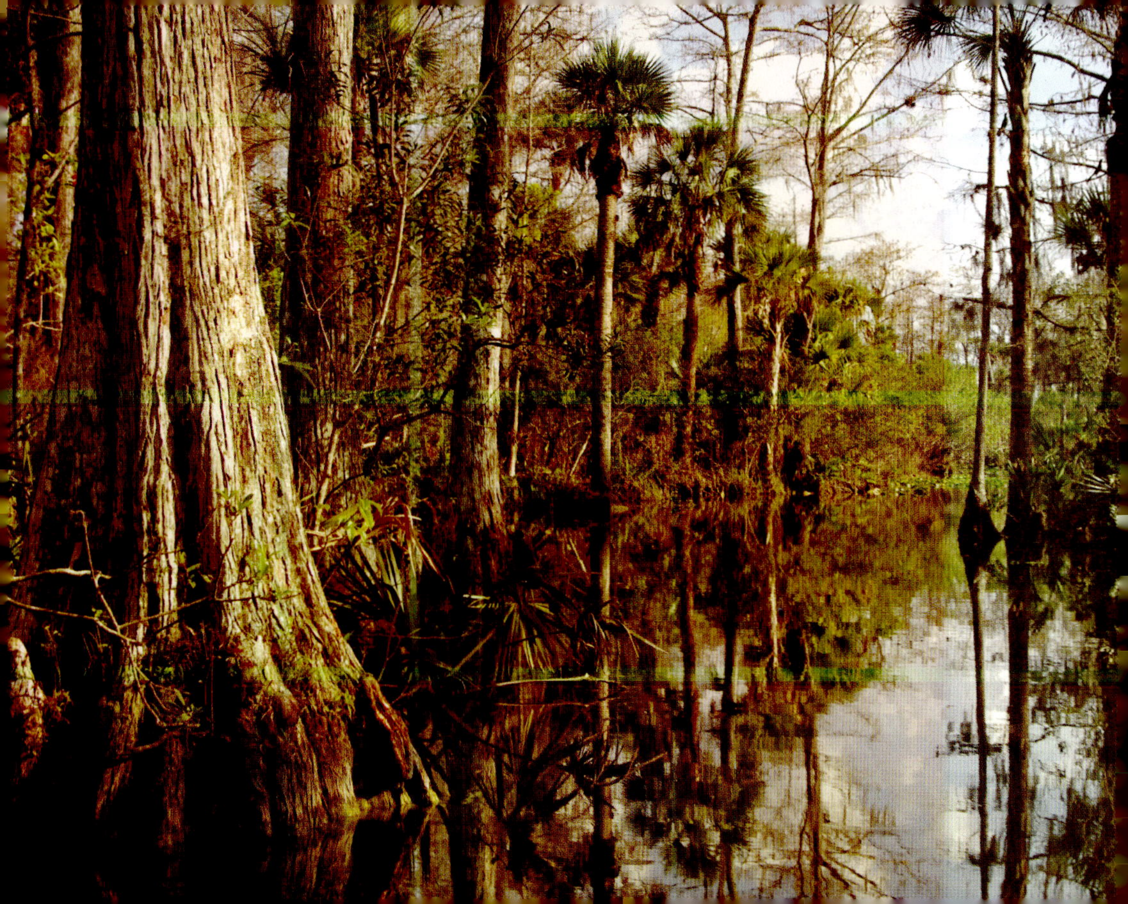

Everglades and the Florida Keys

The Everglades is a national park in south Florida comprising tropical wetlands as part of a drainage basin for waters that start as far north as the Kissimmee River near Orlando in the centre of the state. It provides habitats for many species, including manatees, alligators, the endangered Florida panther, and unwelcome squatters such as pythons, discarded as unwanted pets. Its 0.6 million hectares (1.5 million acres) of sometimes brackish waters have also been designated a World Heritage Site, a Wetland of International Importance and an International Biosphere Reserve.

Further south, the Florida Keys are islands forming a coral archipelago that divides the Atlantic from the Gulf of Mexico and which stretch for 24km (15 miles) south of Miami to Key West, the southernmost point in the United States. Made famous by the film *Key Largo* and the writing of Ernest Hemingway, the Keys are known for their relaxed maritime and party lifestyle, as well as their great natural beauty.

OPPOSITE:
Everglades swamp
Cypress trees wet their knees in the waters of the Everglades.

ALL PHOTOGRAPHS:
Big Cyprus Reservation
One of the six reservations of the Seminole Native American tribe, the reservation is deep in the Everglades, and is the largest one. It is also home to the twelfth-largest cattle ranch in the US, as well as facilities for major entertainment and rodeo shows.

In 1997, the tribe opened the Ah-Tah-Tih-Ki Museum, which became the first tribal museum accredited by the American Association of Museums. The Seminoles are also the only Native American tribe to never sign a peace treaty with the US government.

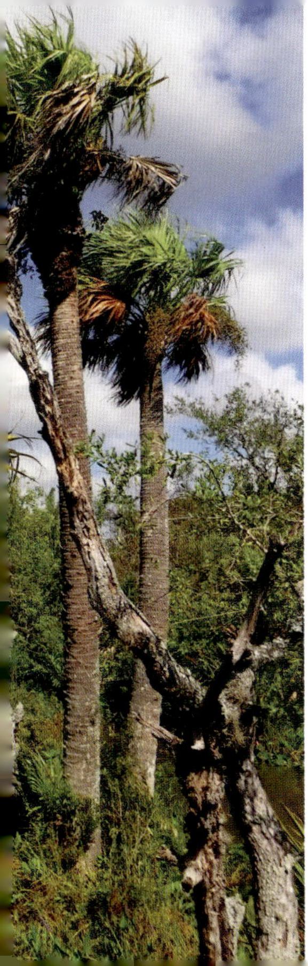

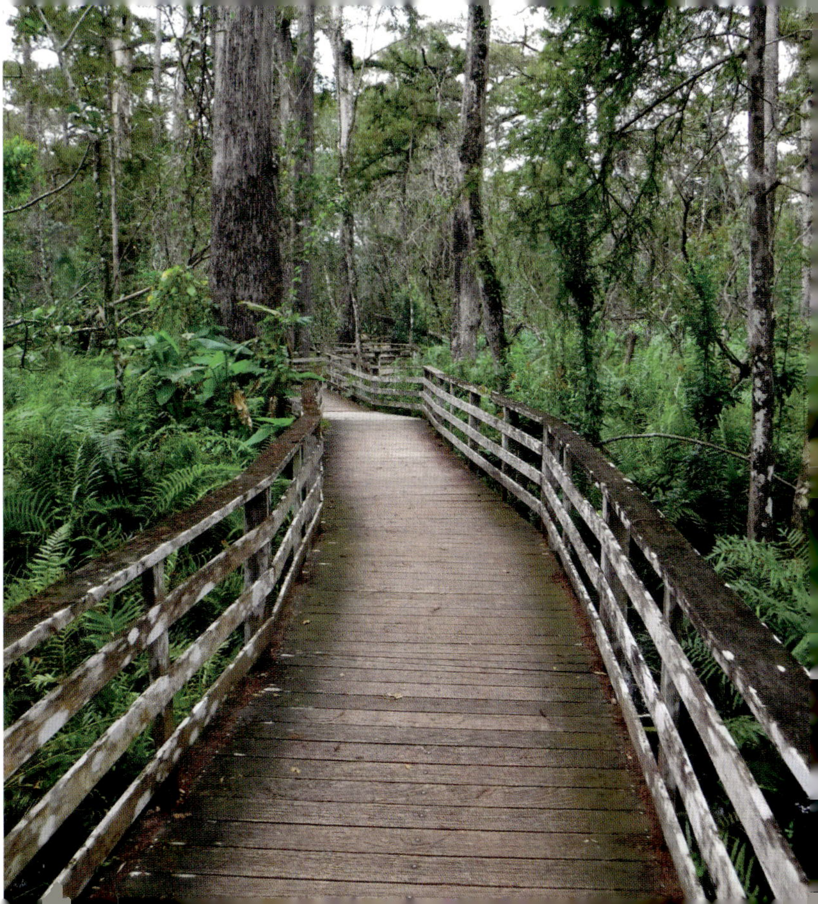

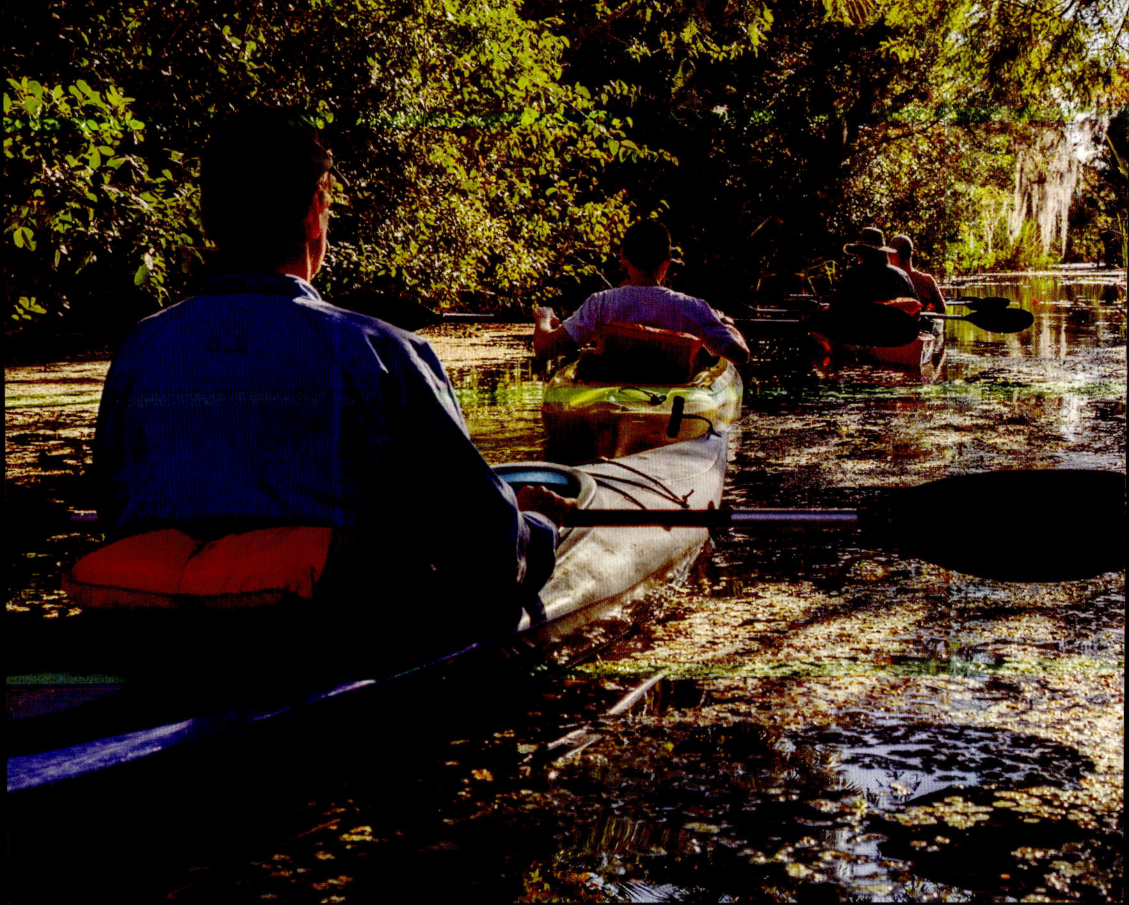

OPPOSITE:

Kayaking, Everglades National Park
There are 12 kayaking routes in the park and adjacent wildlife refuges, and it is an effective and environmentally friendly way to see the area.

RIGHT:

Alligators, Everglades National Park
Alligator mississippienis thrives in the Everglades despite it being the southernmost limit of their territory. As they lack the glands to handle saltwater that crocodiles have, the freshwater swamp suits them. The alligators' skin is darkened in tone by the tannin-rich waters created by the rotting foliage.

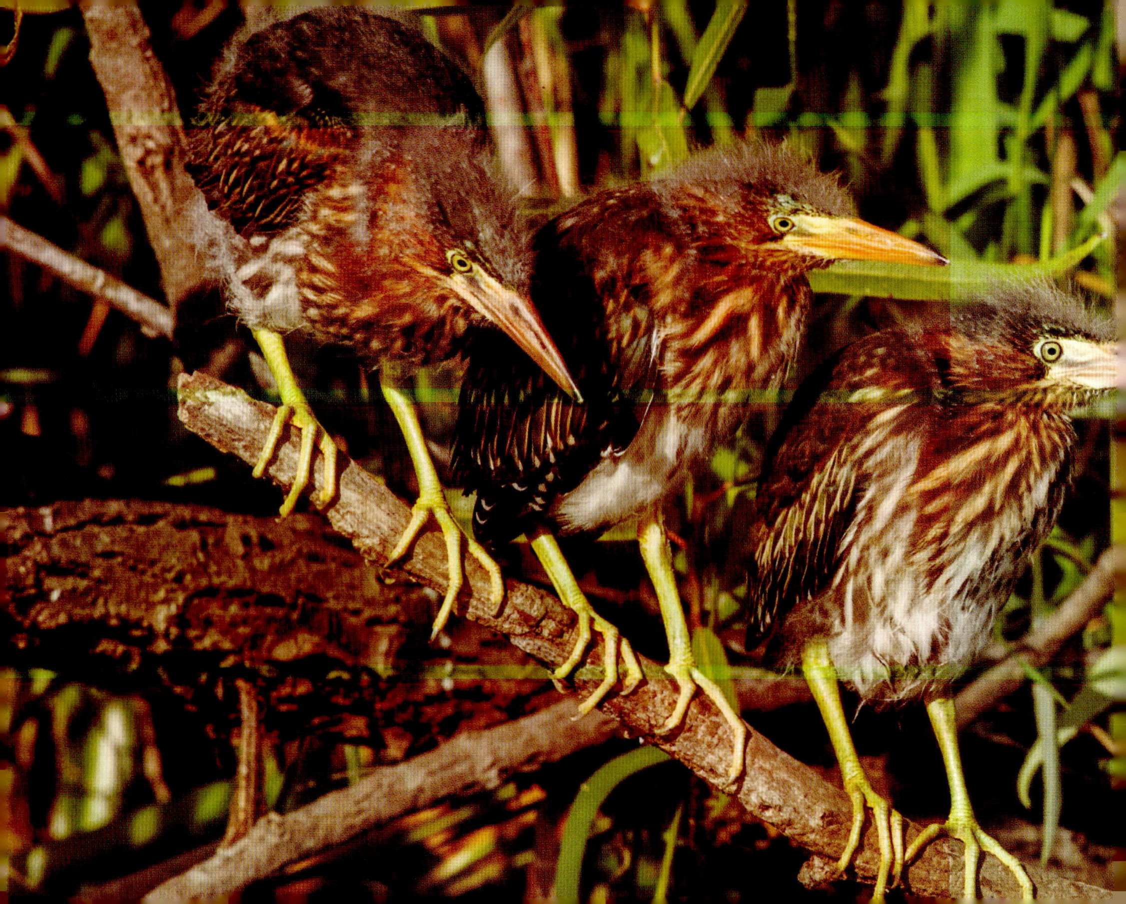

ALL PHOTOGRAPHS:

Wildlife, Everglades National Park
Heron chicks sit on a branch at Shark Valley, while a baby alligator shows its yellow stripes. Racoons (left) will eat alligator eggs.

ABOVE AND OPPOSITE:
Everglades waterways
Officially 159km (99 miles) long, there are many more miles of side inlets. It's about an eight-day journey from the Gulf Coast Visitor Center to the Flamingo Visitors Center at the extreme southern end.

RIGHT:
West Indian manatee
Large and slow, the manatee spends eight hours a day eating plants. Popular with humans because of their perceived friendly personalities, they have had a long struggle back from the edge of extinction.°

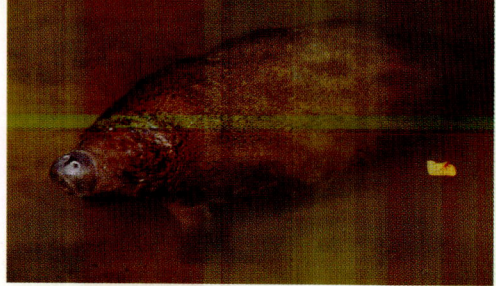

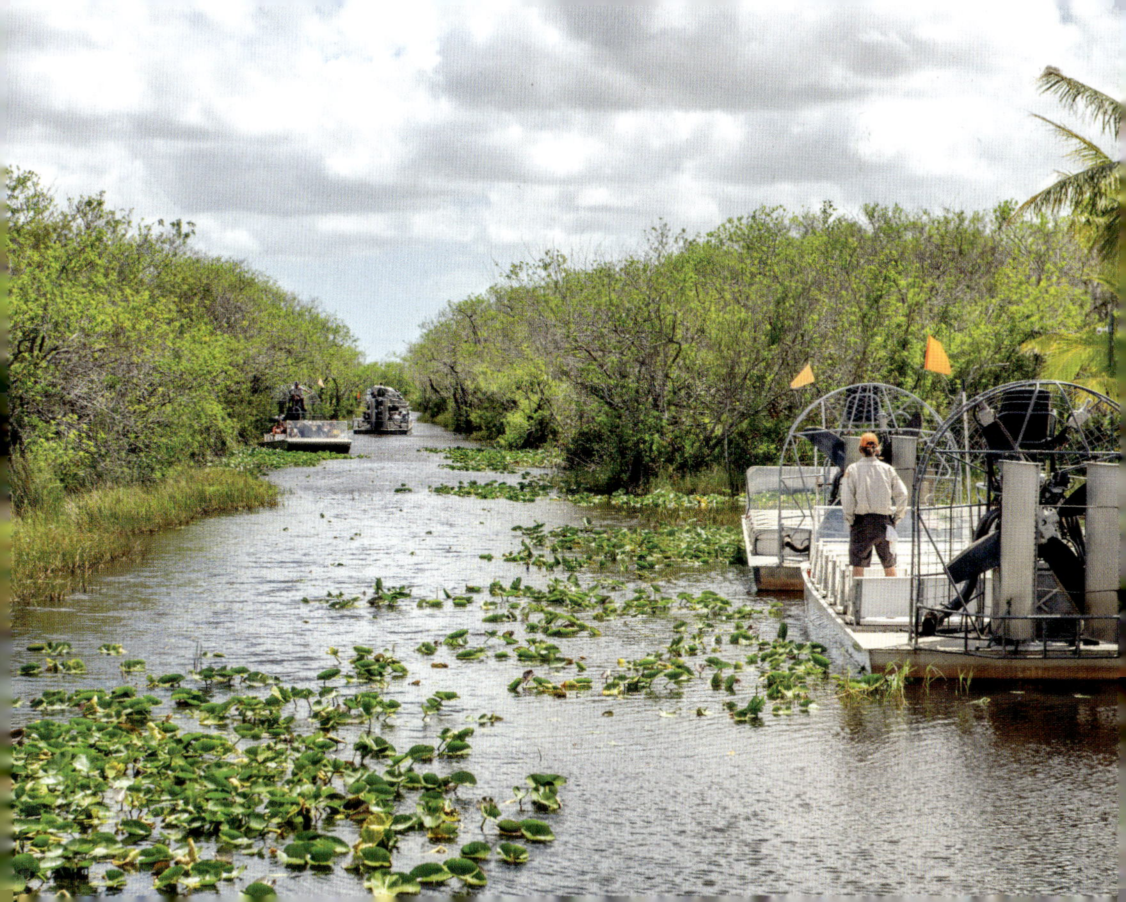

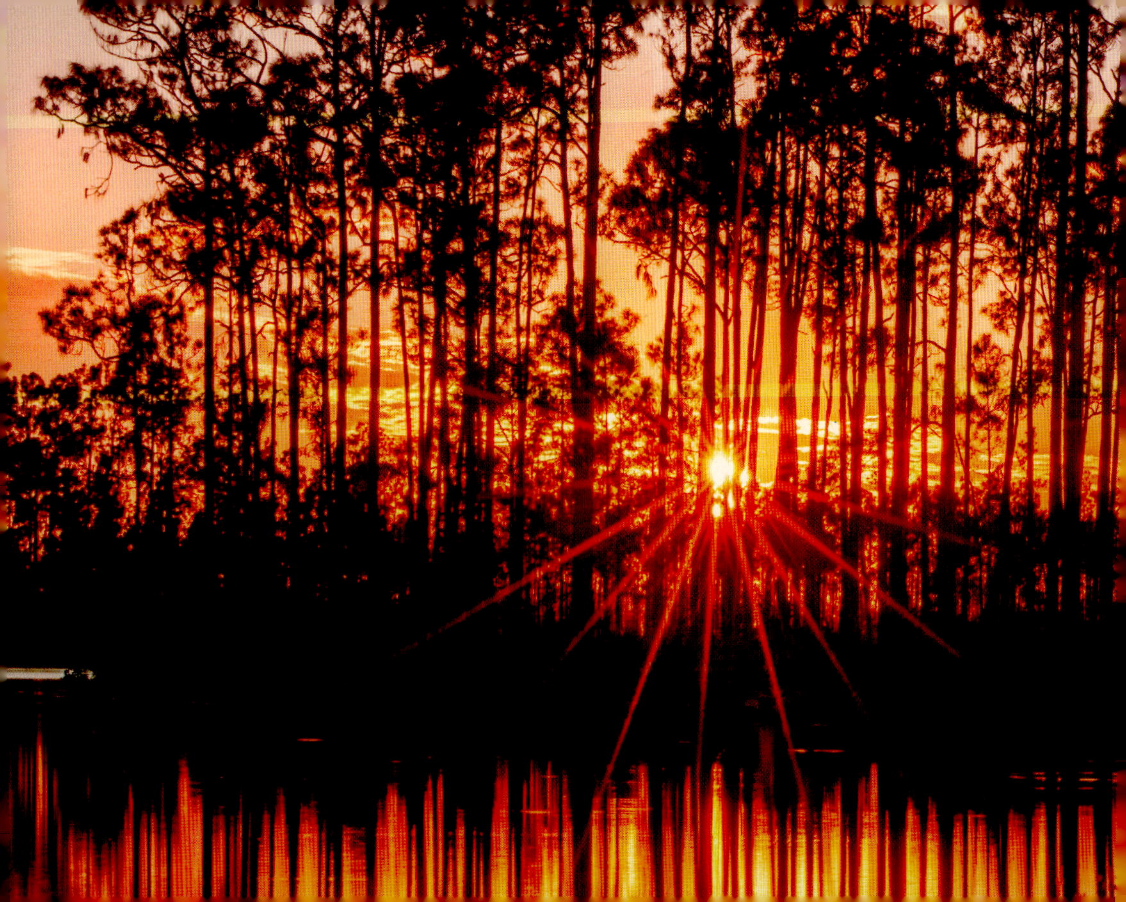

LEFT:
Sunset in the Everglades
The quite breathtaking beauty of the park can be particularly appreciated at sunset and sunrise, with the reflections off the water highlighting the starkness of the trees.

LEFT OVERLEAF:
Brown pelicans, Key Largo
Extraordinarily graceful in flight, they appear clumsy on the ground and often have little that appears brown about them, sometimes having grey or white bodies. If you see one that is almost totally brown it is probably a young bird.

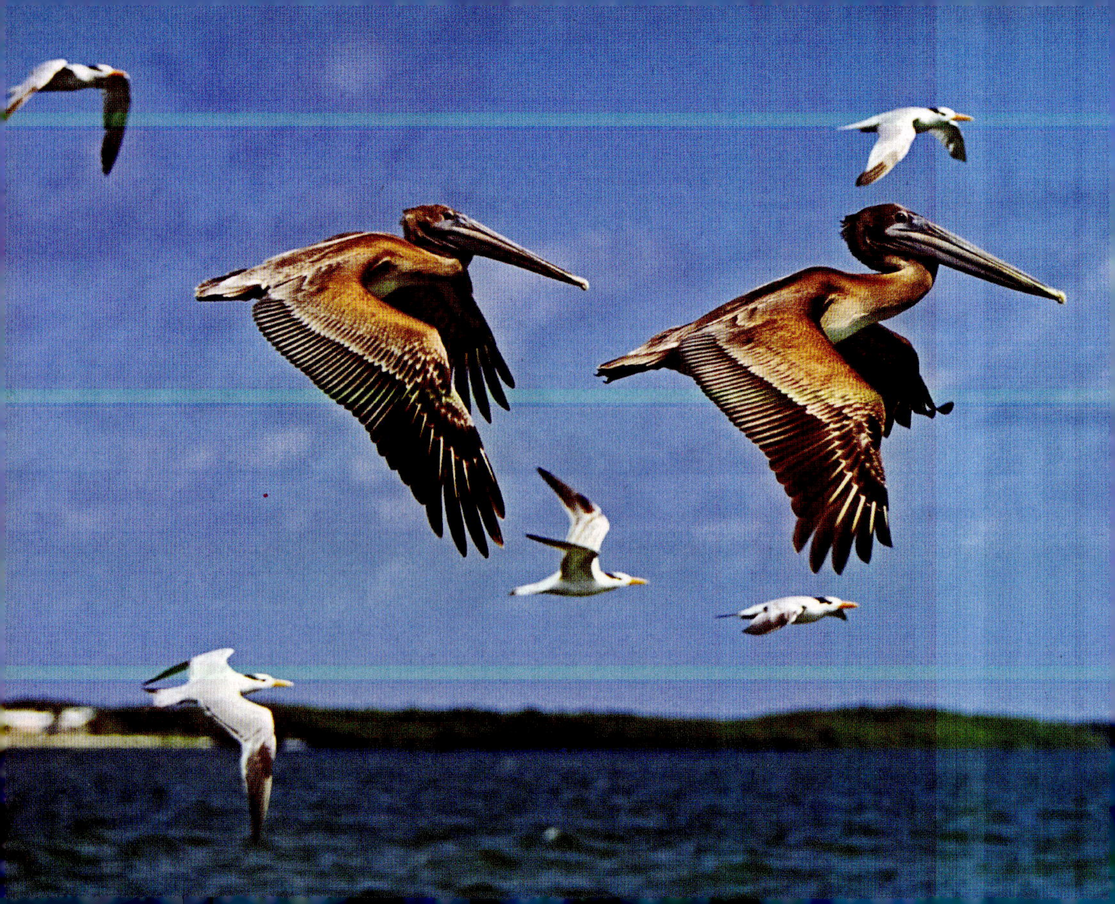

ABOVE:
USS *Spiegel Grove* shipwreck, Key Largo
Purposely sunk in 2002 as part of a manmade reef ecosystem (it sank on its own, six hours before its planned scuttling) the ship was righted on the ocean floor by Hurricane Dennis three years later and is now a popular dive location.

OVERLEAF:
Mangroves, Key Largo
Only found between latitudes of 32 degrees north and 38 degrees south, these unusual salt-tolerant evergreens provide egg laying protection for fish and birds and help prevent the silting up of marine habitats as their roots act as filters.

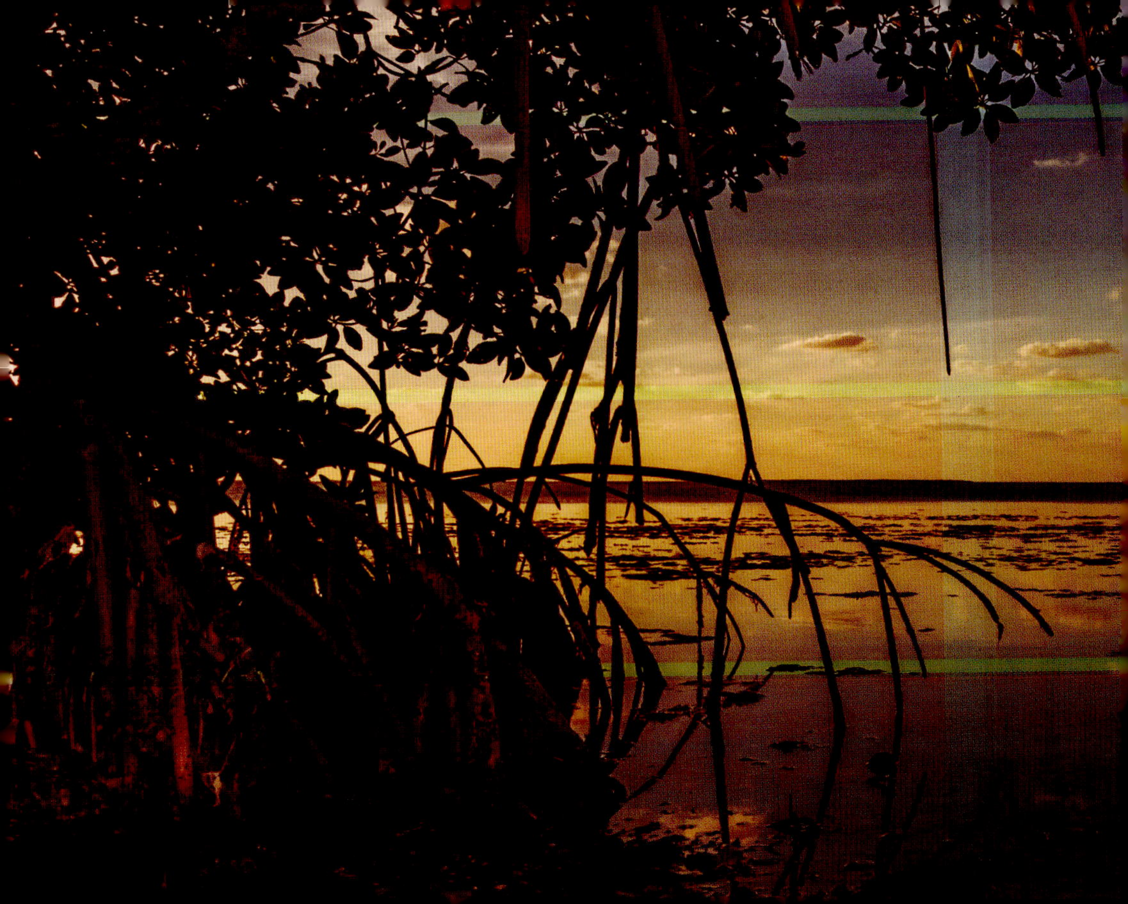

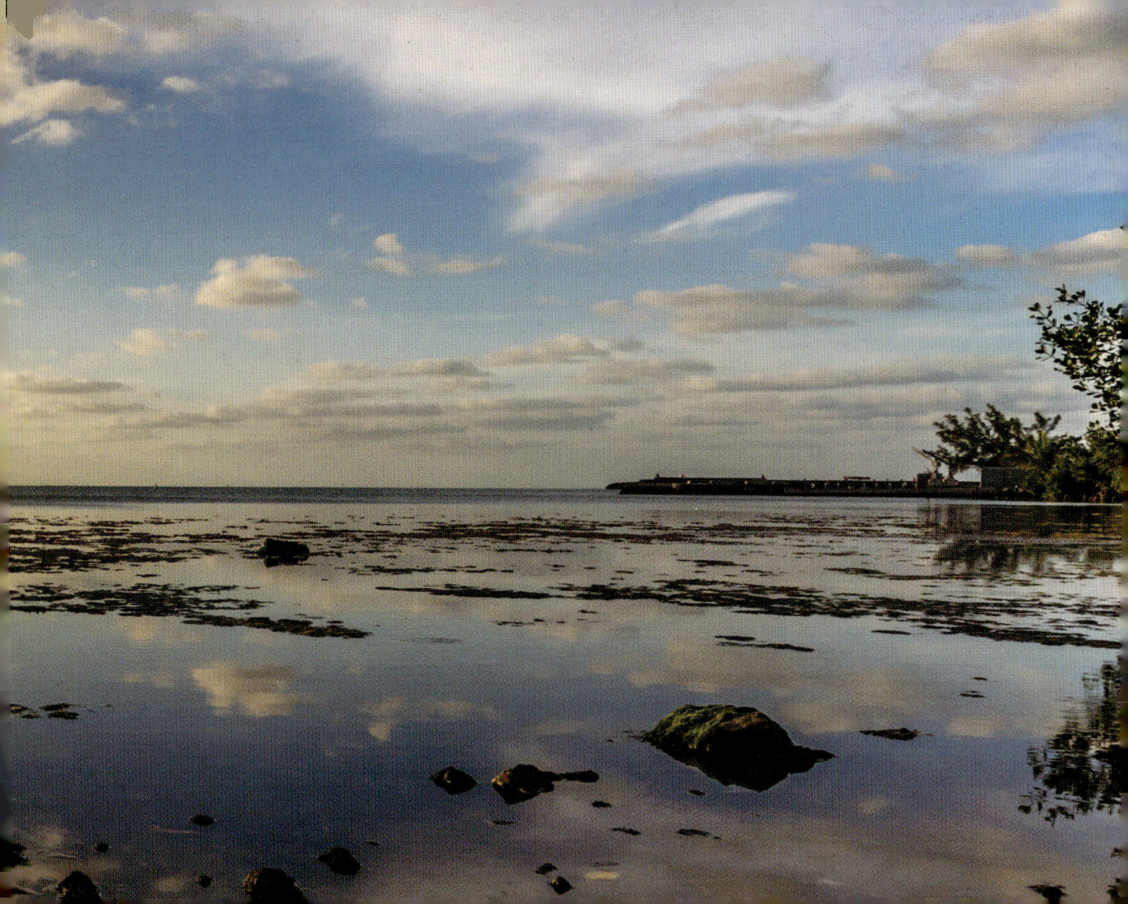

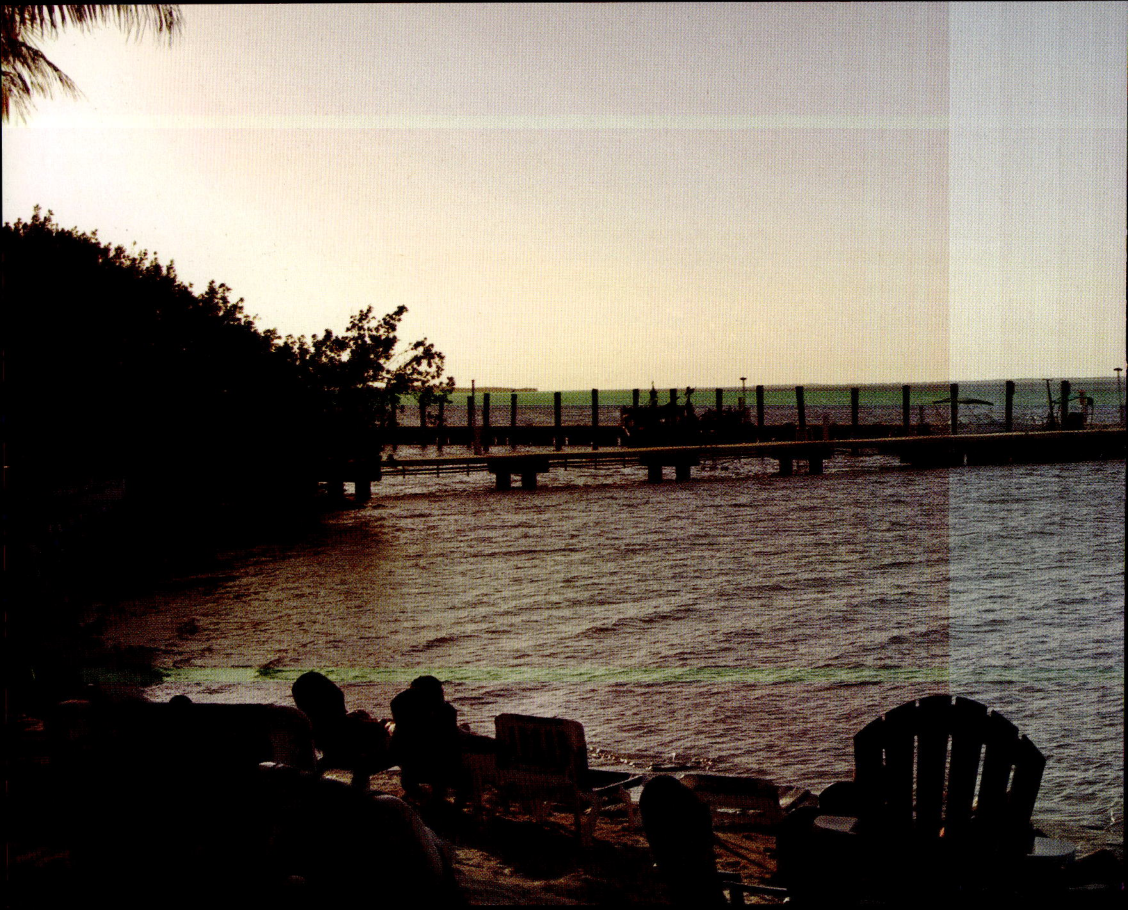

LEFT:
Sunset, Key Largo
A brisk business is done by local tour boats showing the beautiful sunsets and sunrises off to their best advantage.

ABOVE:
Key Largo reef
Multiple reefs exist off the coast of the Key. Diving expeditions can be experienced on many of them.

Marina, Key Largo
There are approximately 39 marinas on Key Largo where visitors can either dock a boat, rent a boat, rent a boat and a skipper, or buy a boat. Some are attached to hotels and resorts, while others are independent. The great fishing and snorkelling off the Keys is well-catered for to, and boats are available in multiple sizes and styles.

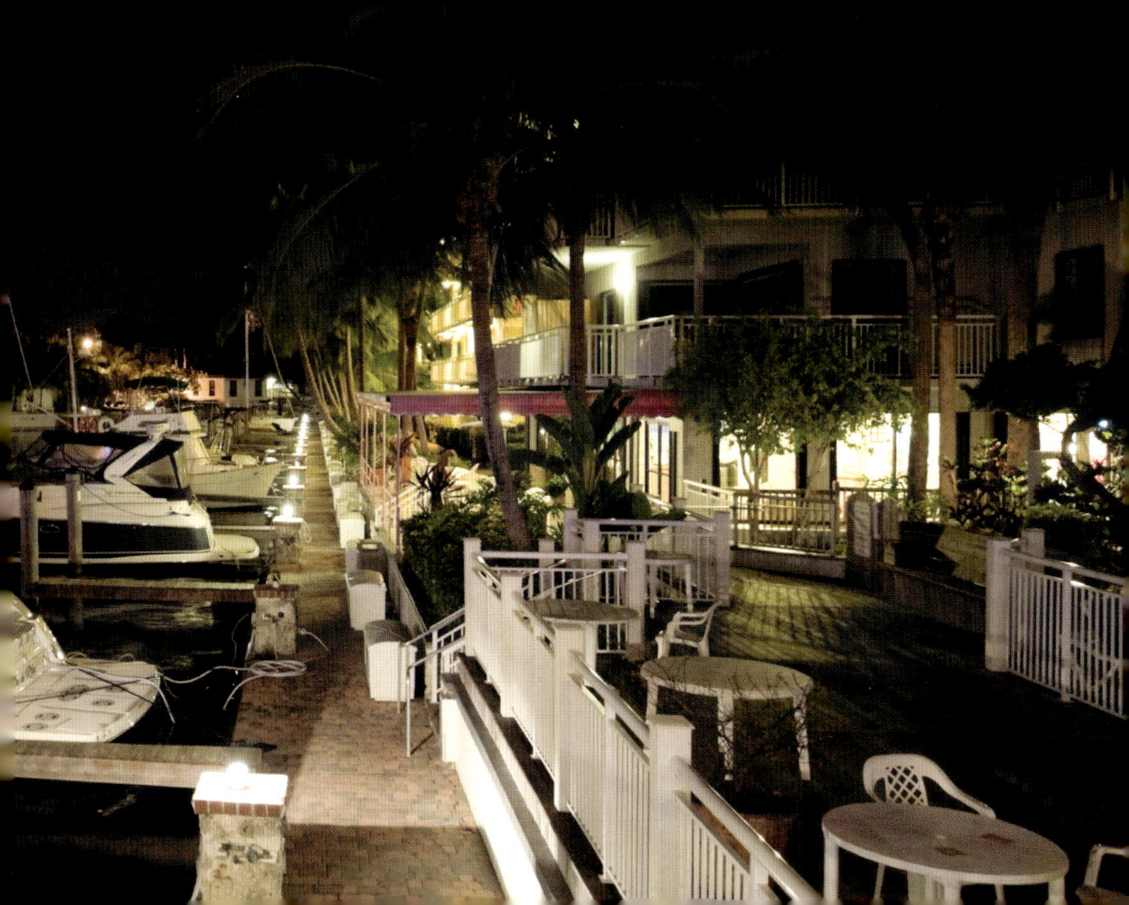

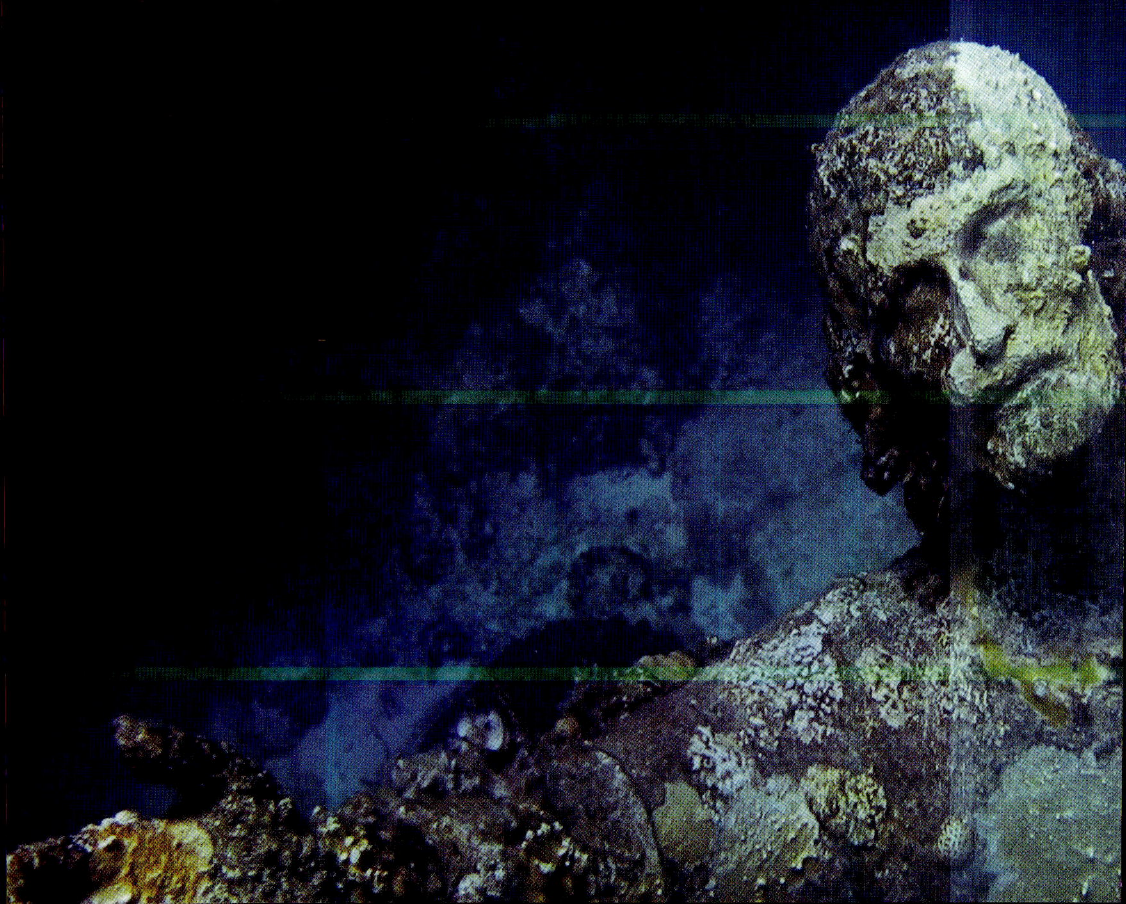

Christ of the Deep Statue, Key Largo
This nearly 2.7m (9ft) high, 13 tonne (29,000lb) bronze statue is the third casting from the original mould (the first is off the coast of Italy, the second is in Grenada). This third casting had a circuitous route to its current underwater site having been first sent to New York, then Chicago, then Orlando, and finally arriving in Key West in 1965.

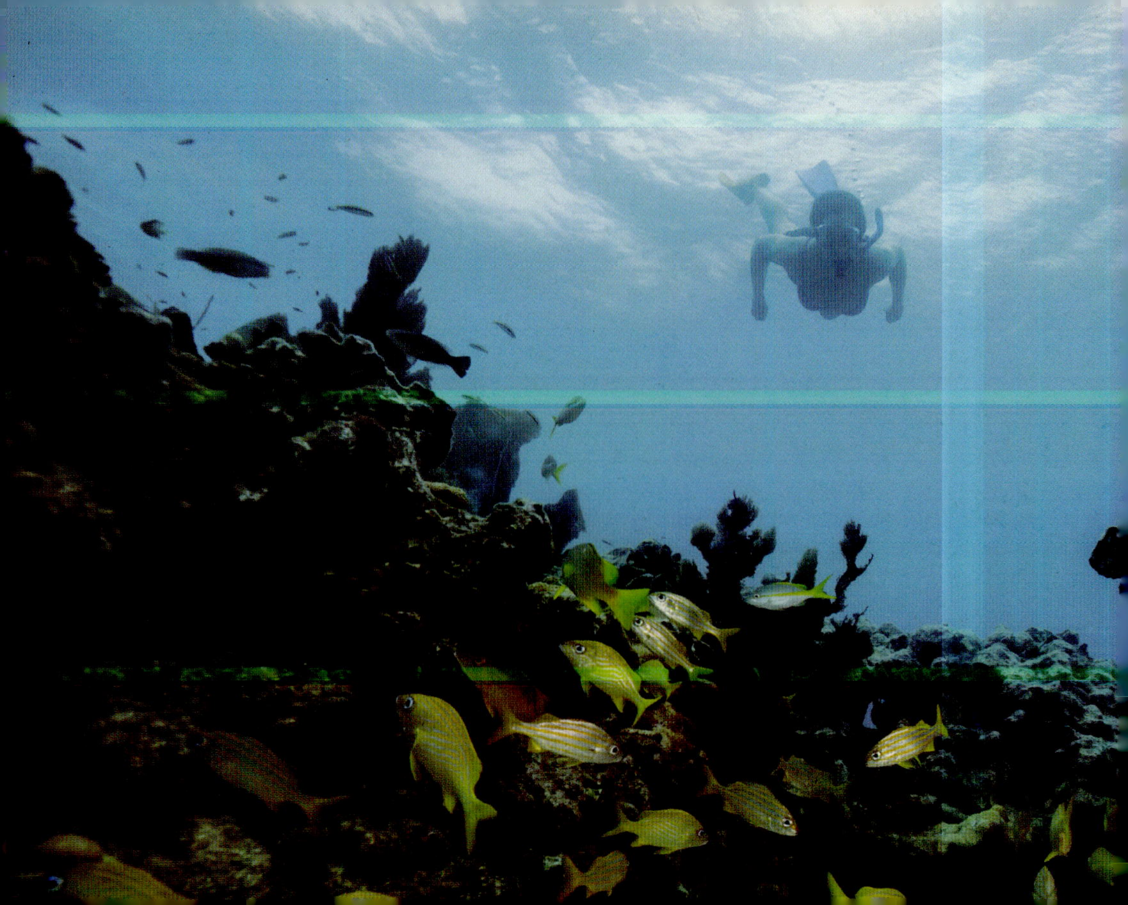

ALL PHOTOGRAPHS:
Coral reef, Key Largo
There are multiple coral reefs around Key Largo, including an underwater park. The usual ways to experience them are by glass-bottomed boat, or by snorkelling or scuba diving.

ABOVE:

Faro Blanco Lighthouse, Marathon

The 20m (65ft) tower was built in 1950 and is now part of the Faro Blanco Resort and Yacht club. Originally a promotional gimmick but actually used as a private aid for navigation, it has been restored after falling into disrepair following repeated hurricane damage over the years.

RIGHT:

Marathon

The city of Marathon sits on 13 islands in the Keys. Renowned for boating, deep-sea fishing and good local restaurants, it lies halfway down from the mainland on the way to Key West.

140

Welcome to MARATHON

ALL PHOTOGRAPHS:
Big Pine Key
Big Pine Key is a community on its namesake island in the Florida Keys and was the site of one of the stations on Henry Flagler's Overseas Railroad. It lies about 37km (23 miles) down Route 1 from Marathon.

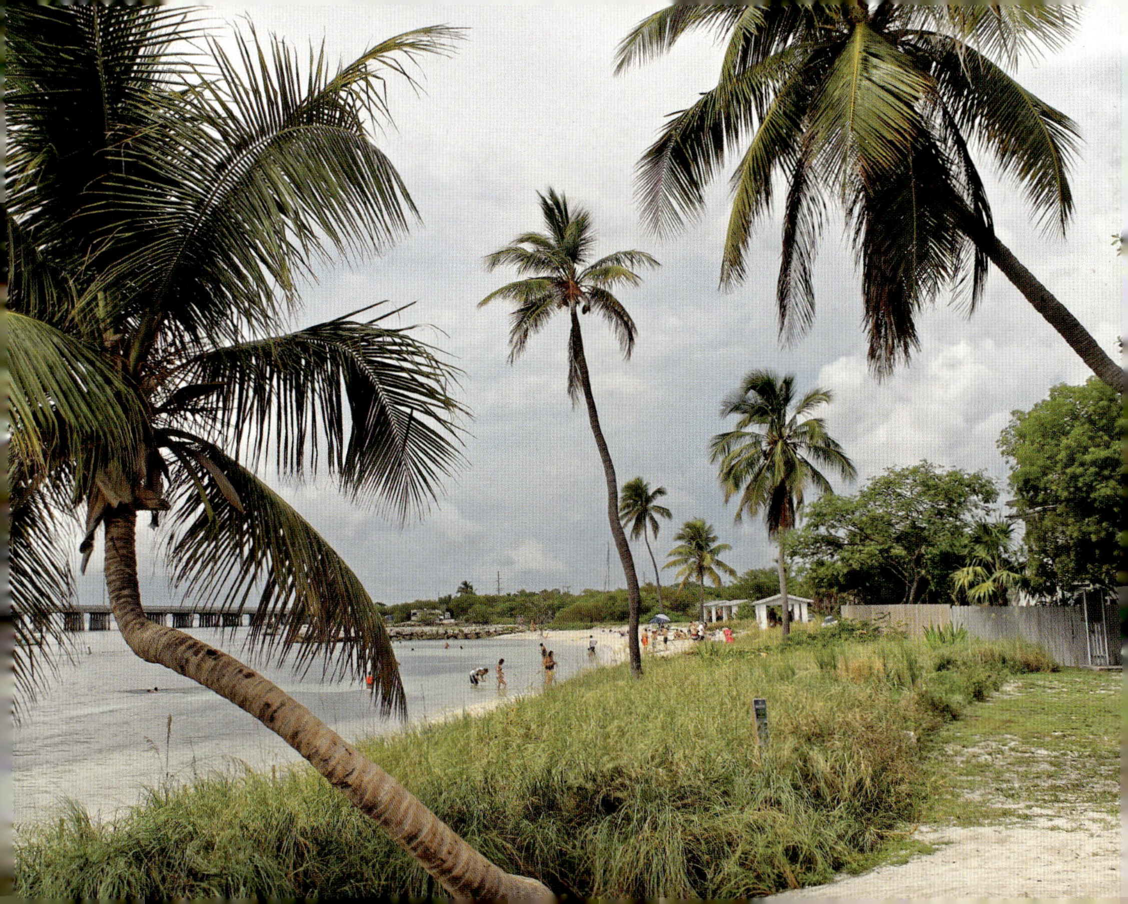

ABOVE:

Key Deer Refuge
Big Pine Key is home to the Key Deer Refuge that is in turn home to most of the endangered Key Deer species.

OPOSITE:

No Name Pub
Three miles off Route 1 is No Name Key, sparsely populated but home to the No Name Pub, one of the world's great bar names and a perfect place to get away from it all.

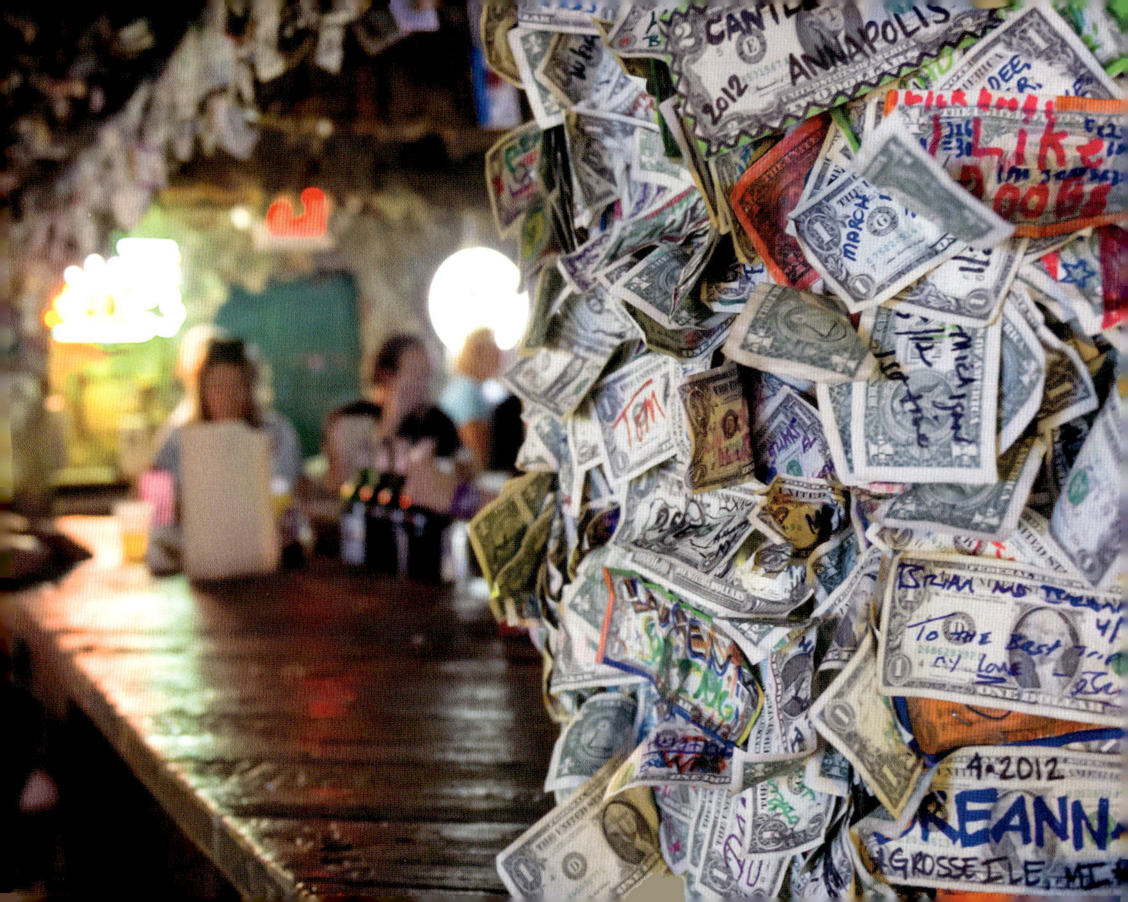

ALL PHOTOGRAPHS:
Key West
The city of Key West, also known as the Conch Republic, includes parts of Dredger's Key, Sunset Key, Fleming Key and Stock Island, as well as the island of Key West. It is also the southernmost place in the continental United States. This bar sports signs reflecting the bohemian island style that has come to be identified with the city.

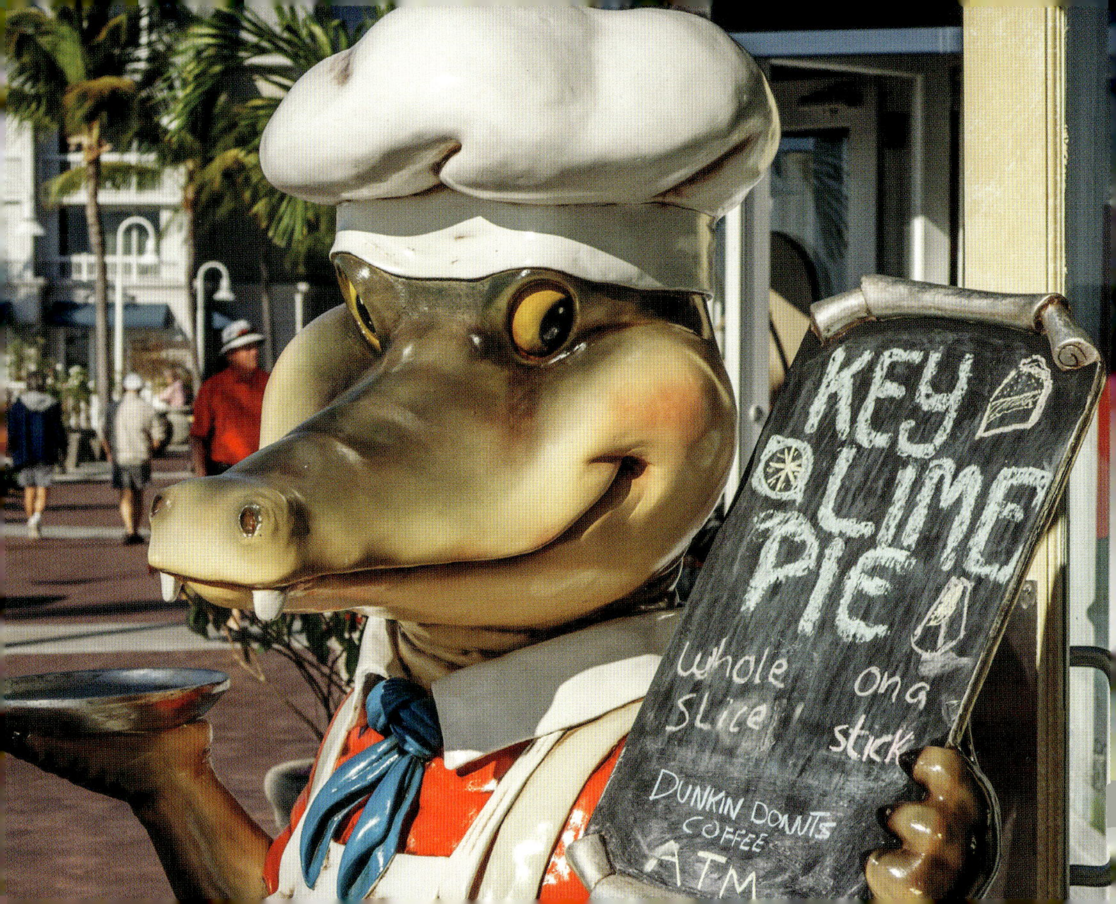
KEY LIME PIE
whole slice
on a stick
DUNKIN DONUTS COFFEE
ATM

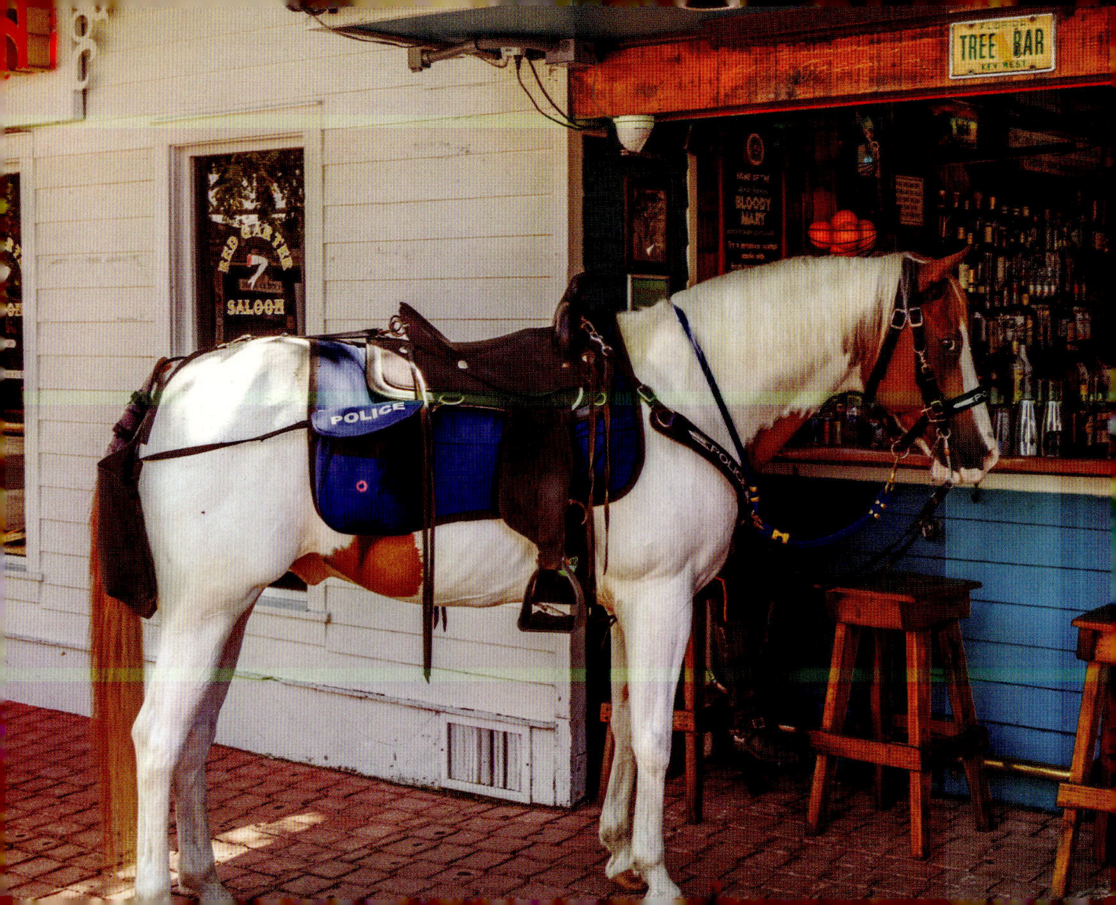
TREE BAR
SALOON
BLOODY MARY
POLICE

OPPOSITE:

Horse at the bar, Key West

As part of the Key West vibe, this bar keeps its own equine visitor.

LEFT:

Key lime pie

Made from Key lime juice, egg yolks, and condensed milk, this dessert is a popular.

ABOVE:

Annual Hemingway Days, Key West

This July celebration of the famous author has a Hemingway look-alike contest that is a bonanza for white-bearded men.

LEFT:

Hemingway the Fisherman, Custom House Museum, Key West

Remembered almost as much for his outdoor pursuits as his writing, Hemingway combined both in *The Old Man and The Sea*. The story is that Hemingway used to load his fishing boat up with guns and hand grenades and go out hunting German U-boats, as well as game fish, during World War II.

RIGHT:

Florida Keys

The Keys include dozens of small uninhabited islets, often in clusters, that can make for some tricky navigation.

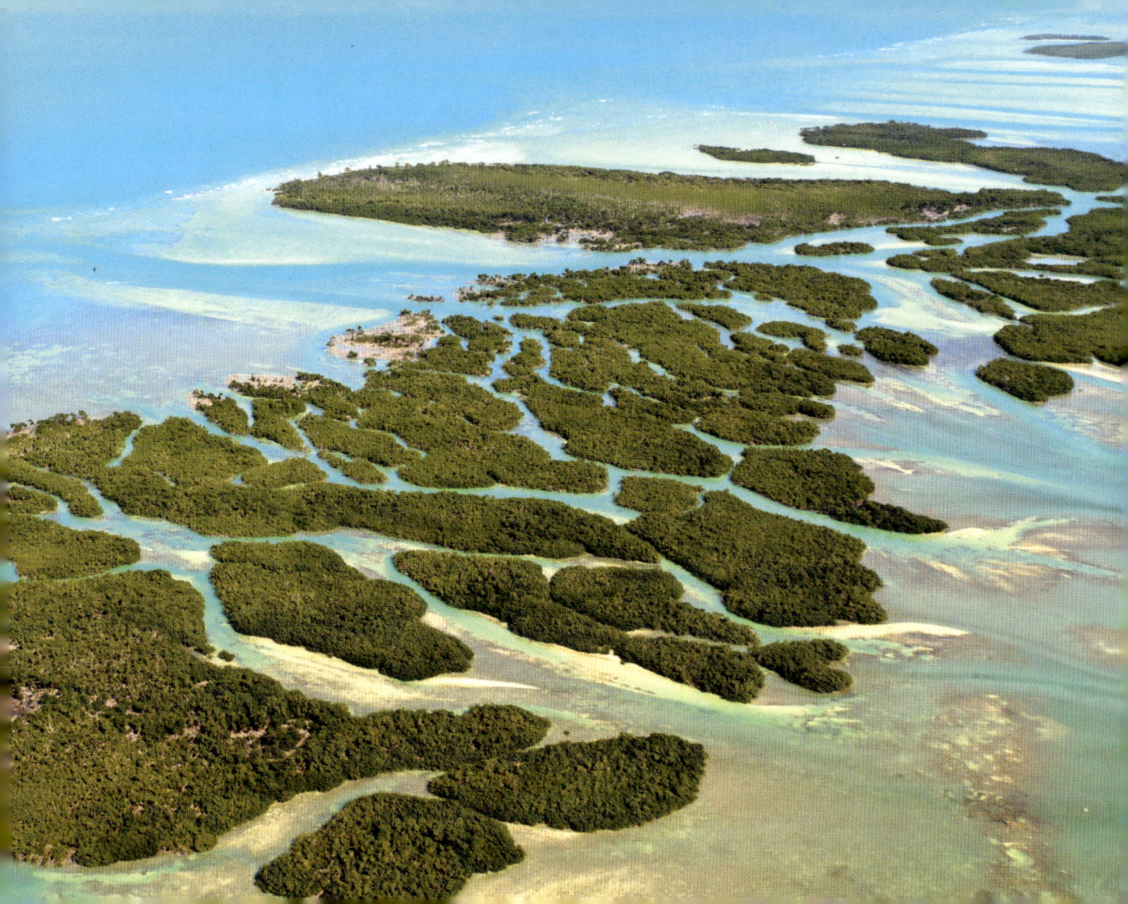

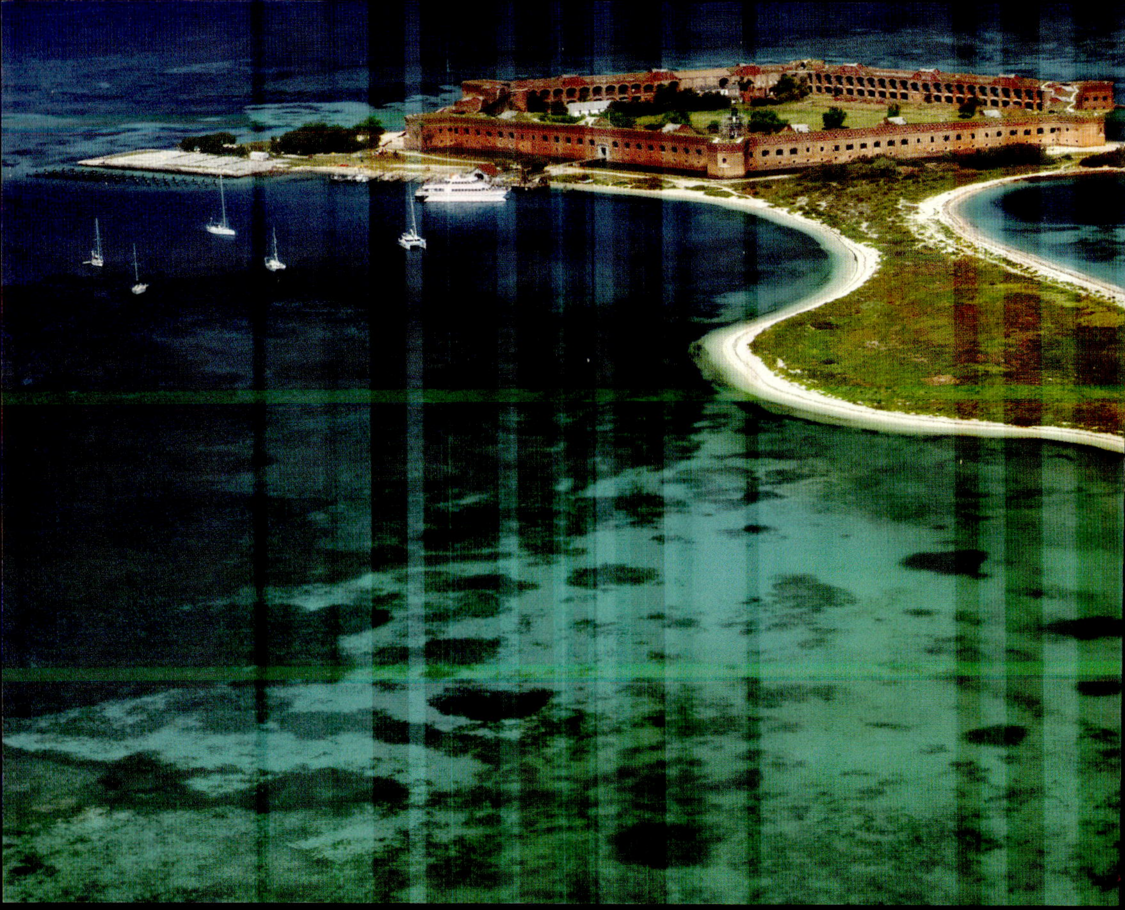

Dry Tortugas National Park
Fort Jefferson, on the westernmost of the Florida Keys, was used as a prison during the American Civil War (1861–65). Today, tourists explore it before going snorkelling in the very clear local waters.

Key West bridges
Seven Mile Bridge is actually two bridges, the old one and the new one. The old one has a section missing but it can still be used to reach Pigeon Key, and is now for foot traffic only. Its guardrails are re-purposed railway lines from the railway that originally crossed the bridge. The new bridge carries traffic.

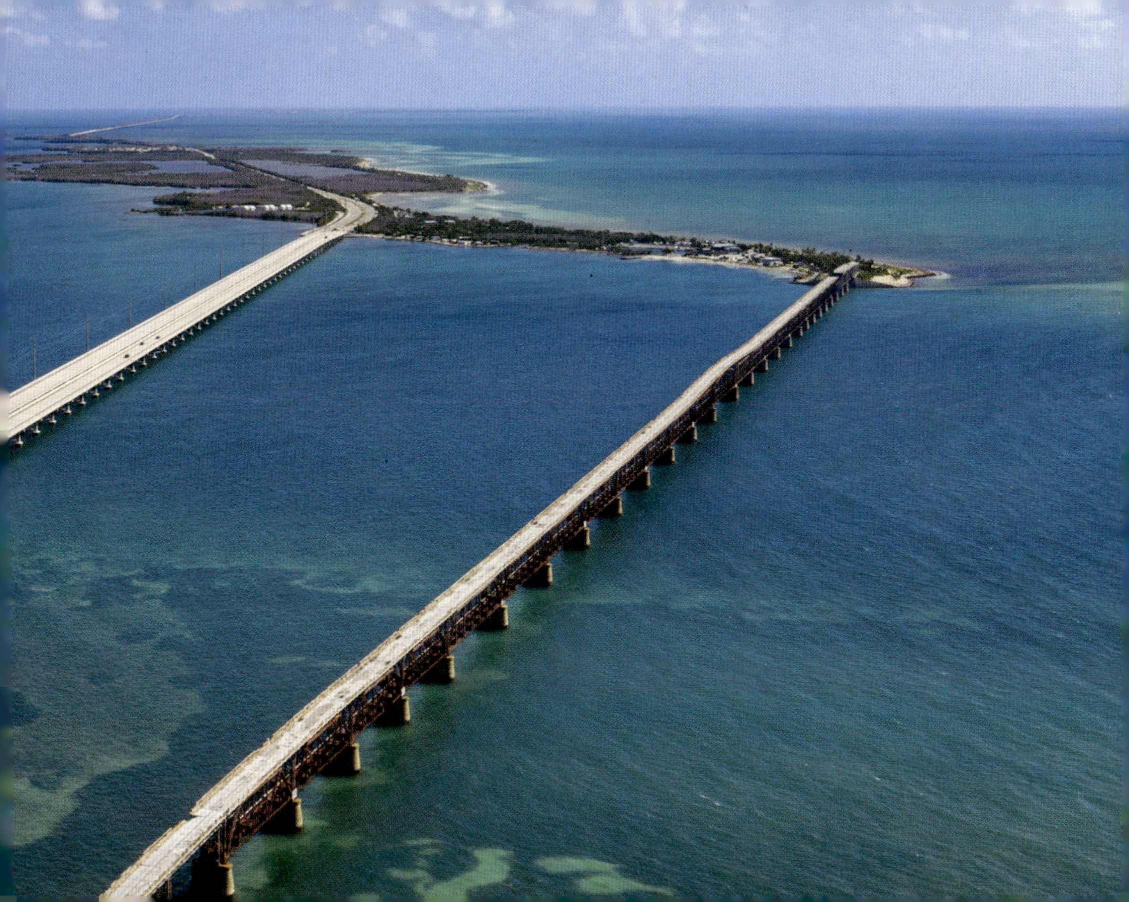

ABOVE:
Bar, Port of Key West
There are 360 liquor licenses in Key West, most attached to bars, and the majority do good business. Captain Tony's is supposedly the oldest, and Sloppy Joe's on Duvall St. possibly the best known. Many are al fresco, taking advantage of the Key's weather.

RIGHT:
Mallory Square, Key West
The Sunset Celebration is a nightly event in Mallory Square, and it draws large crowds there to view the sun going down.

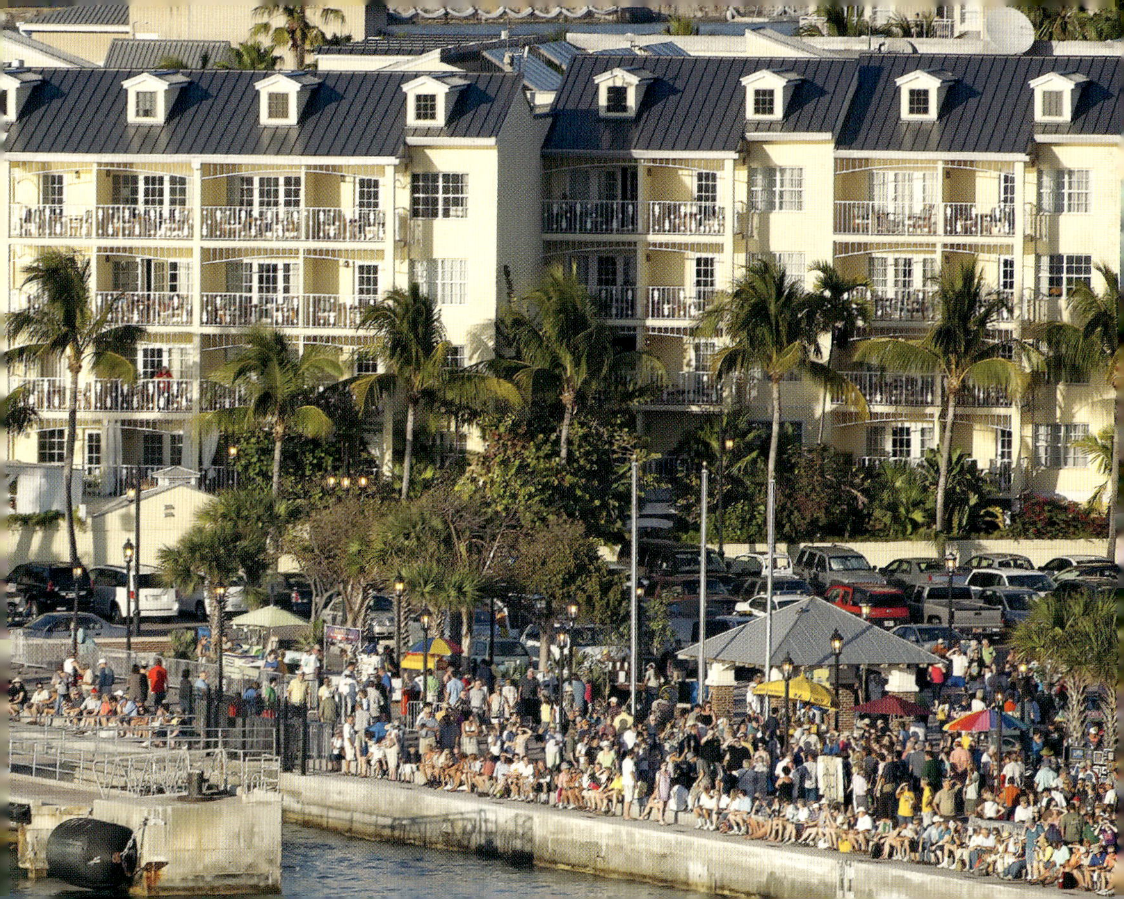

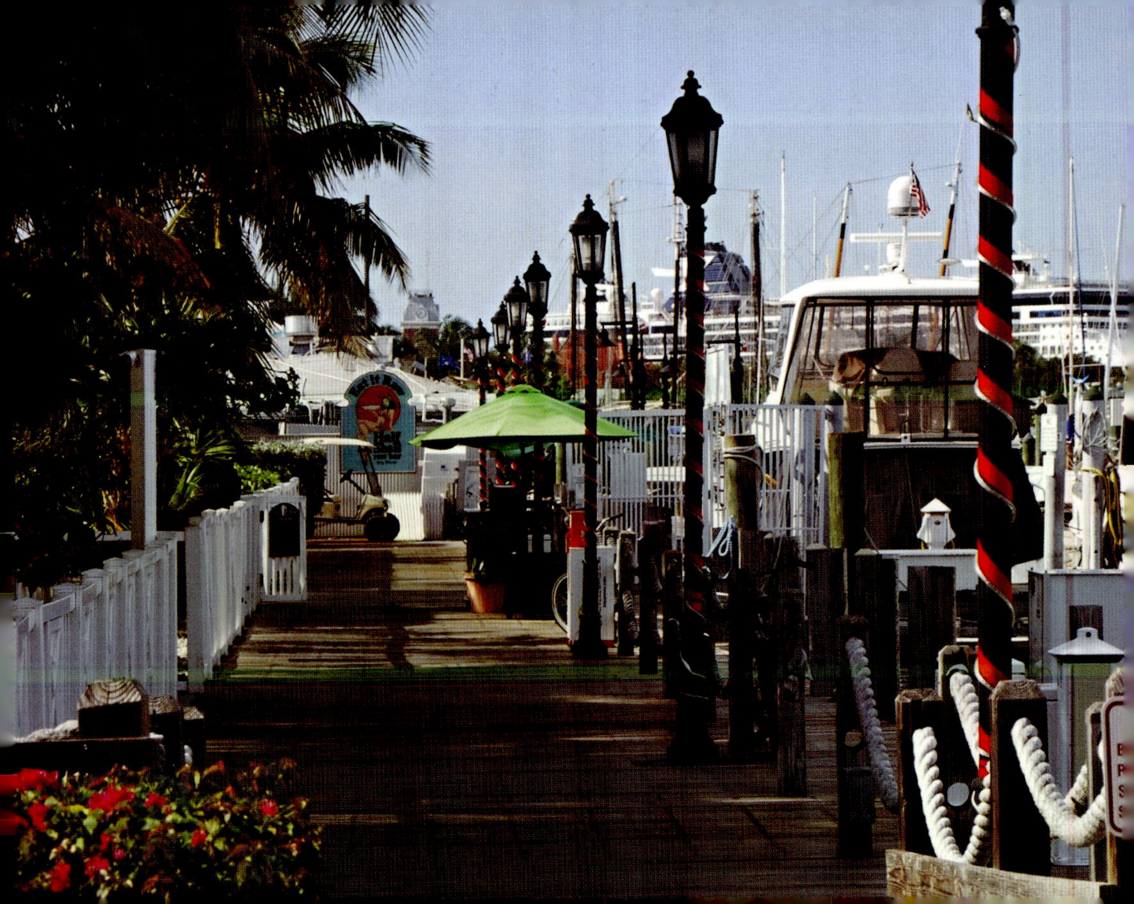

LEFT:

Marina, Key West

The Key West Bight Marina is in the middle of the historic district at the old seaport. There are 12 other marinas, including the one on Stock Island.

ABOVE:

Entertainment, Key West

Many of the bars in Key West feature live entertainment, usually music. Bars must close by 4.00am so there is plenty of time to sing and dance the night away.

THE CONCH REPUBLIC
90 Miles to
CUBA
SOUTHERNMOST
POINT
CONTINENTAL
U.S.A.
KEY WEST, FL
Home of the Sunset

LEFT AND ABOVE:
Southernmost Point Buoy, Key West
Located at the corner of Whitehead Street and South Street the buoy marking the southernmost point in the continental United States is a co-star of uncountable holiday snaps and selfies.

OVERLEAF:
Sea turtles
Key West is home to four types of sea turtles: loggerhead, hawksbill, ridley and green.

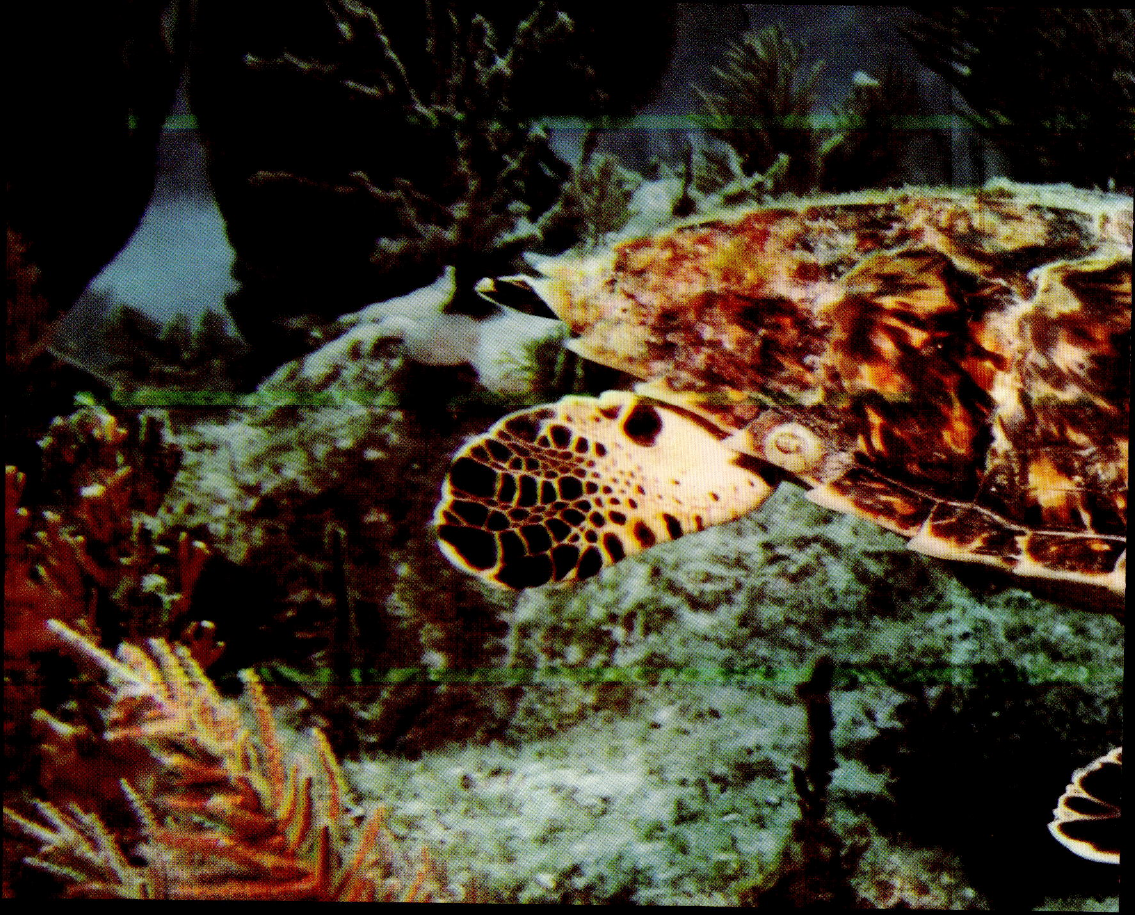

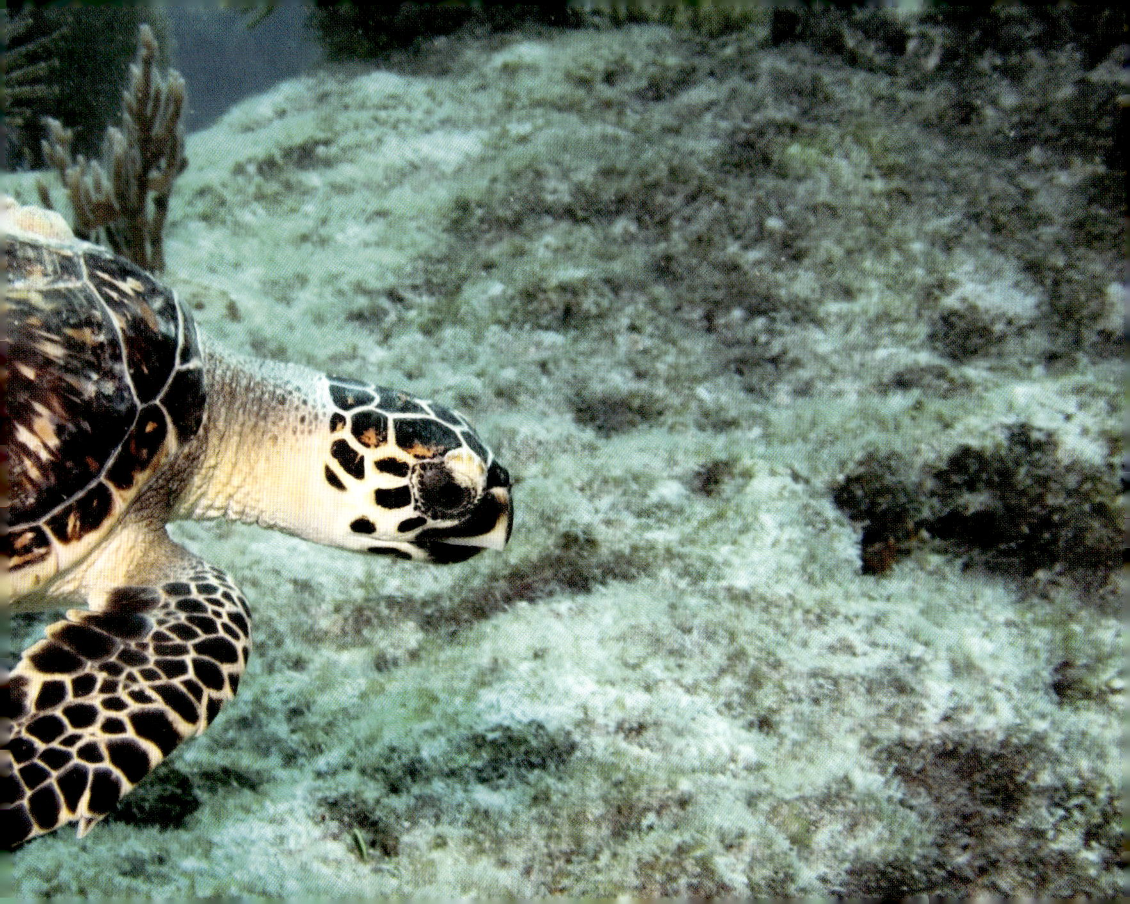

PLEASURE ISLAND

Orlando and Around

Orlando, 'The City Beautiful', is the third-largest metropolitan area in Florida, after Miami and Tampa. It is best known as the home of Walt Disney World and Universal Studios Florida, but there is a great deal more to it. A major international tourism destination, it draws up to of 75 million visitors a year.

The Orlando area was part of a Seminole Native American reservation, but the Indian Removal Act of 1830 sent the Seminoles to Oklahoma, after which the area was called Jernigan, after a family of early settlers. The city grew out of a US Army post called Fort Gatlin, built in 1838 as part of the Second Seminole War.

There are many theories on the origin of the Orlando name, one being a tribute to the Shakespeare character in *As You Like It*, the other referring to Orlando Reeves, whose grave marker was prominent in the area. There are many other variations on these two stories.

Cattle ranching and citrus fruit farming were early local industries and tourism came at the end of the 19th century. Orlando benefitted from the Florida Land Boom of the 1920s and 30s but the biggest boost for came from the city fathers convincing the government to route Interstate 4 through the area instead of Tampa, as had been originally envisioned.

OPPOSITE:

Pleasure Island, Walt Disney World

Pleasure Island is part of Downtown Disney, the free-to-enter section adjacent to the parks that was originally built to compete with downtown Orlando's nightlife.

ALL PHOTOGRAPHS:
Downtown Orlando
The city is a mixture of modern high-rise office blocks and older historic buildings, and has many attractive residential districts, such as College Park and Thornton Park. As well as a new stadium, the city has major basketball and hockey franchises.

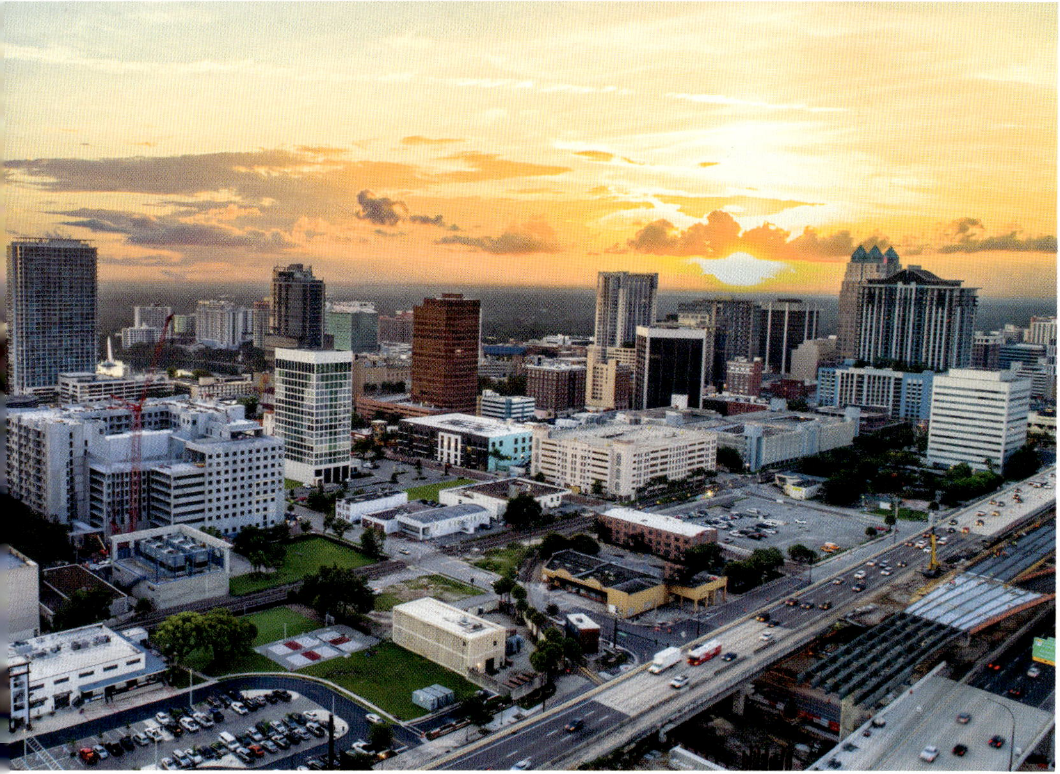

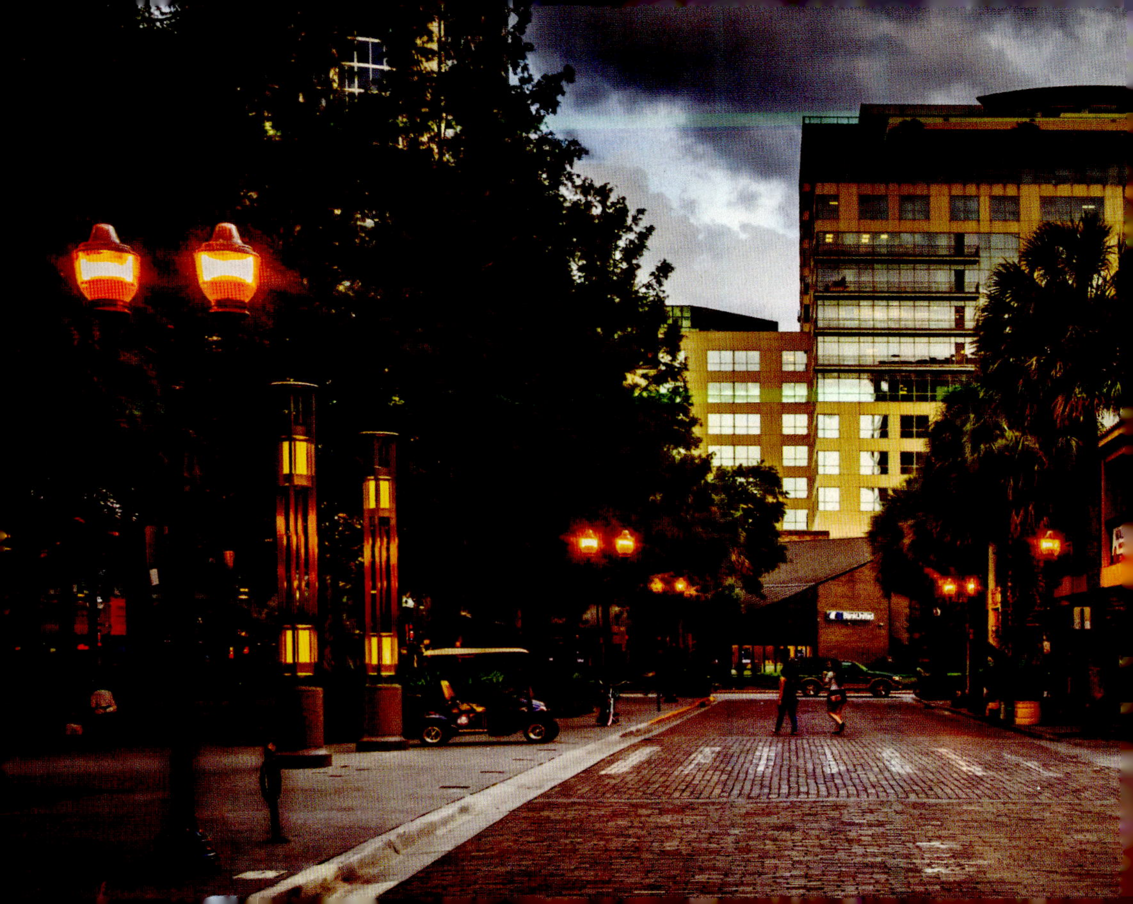

Wall Street, downtown Orlando
The Wall Street area between Lake Eola and Orange Avenue has multiple bars and restaurants, and frequent outdoor concerts and events. At weekends, the area is busy with young bar-hoppers, mostly locals. Brick Street is very close to the Smithsonian affiliated Orange County Regional History Center, which features rotating exhibitions of local art and subjects of local historical interest.

ALL PHOTOGRAPHS:
Lake Eola, Orlando
Located right in the middle of the downtown area, the lake has fountains, attractive lighting and a partially wooded surround. It is a great place for a walk, or to visit one of the weekend markets or surrounding bars or restaurants. There are regular concerts and every Christmas there is a free performance of Tchaikovsky's *Nutcracker* that draws large crowds of locals.

171

ABOVE:

Lake Eola birdlife
As well as black swans, visitors to the lake will also find geese, pelicans, herons and other species who come for the cracked corn on sale.

RIGHT:

Orlando City skyline
The lake is a perfect vantage point from which to view the downtown skyline, which is lit up at night.

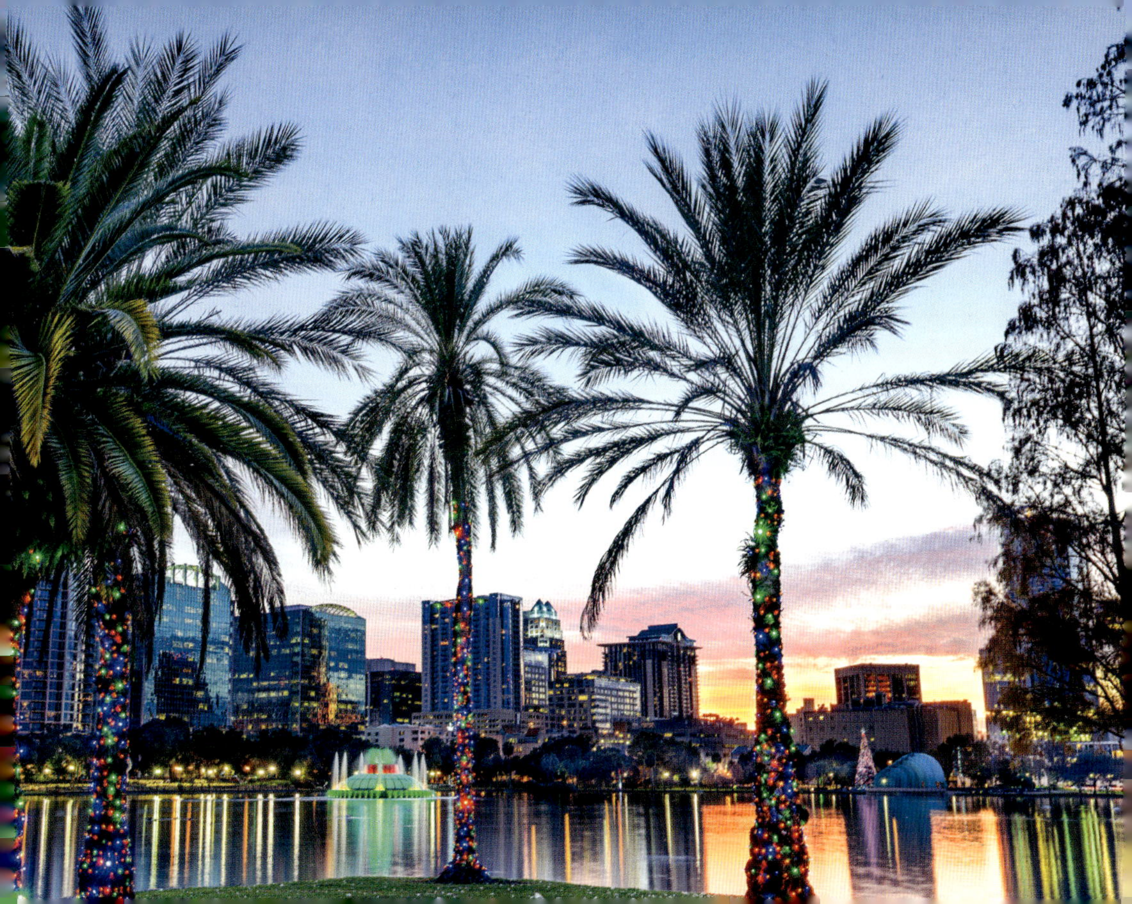

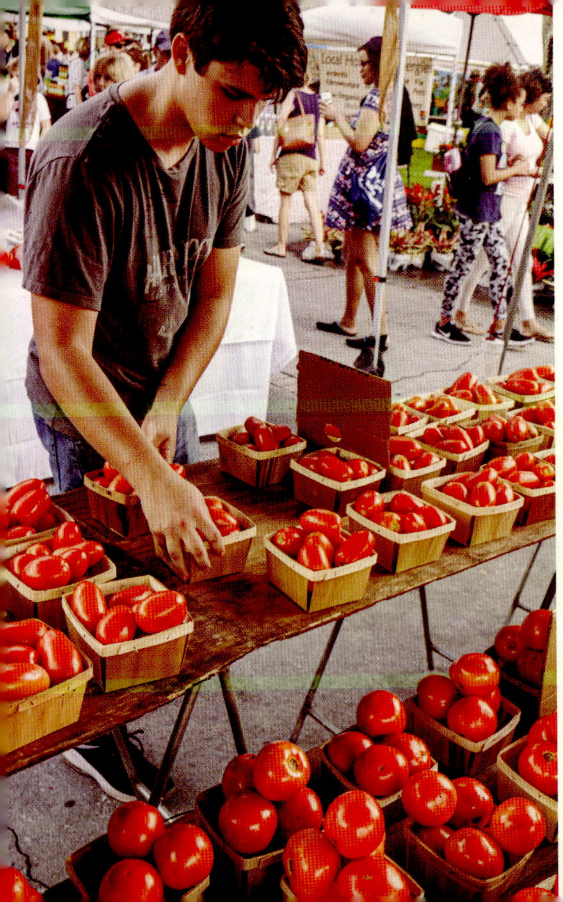

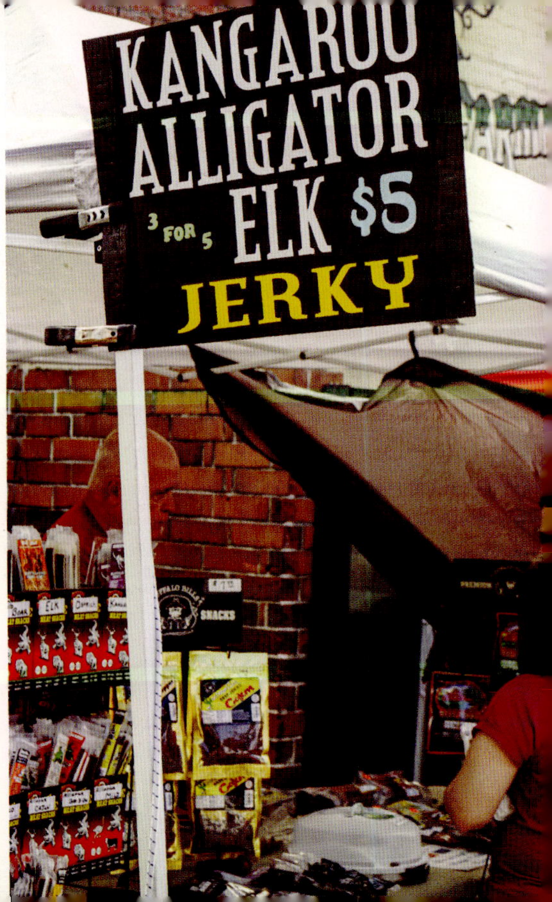
KANGAROO
ALLIGATOR
3 FOR 5
ELK $5
JERKY

ALL PHOTOGRAPHS:
Lake Eola Farmers' Market
Open on Sundays, this popular market features fresh local produce, artisanal food, carnival-type foods such as funnel cake, and even a bouncy castle. It gets busy and has an atmosphere more like a county fair than a farmers' market.

Mi. Celery
$1.50
Each
Ga. Beet Greens
$2.50
each
Mi. Gold Beets
$1.99 lb.

ALL PHOTOGRAPHS:
Farmers' markets, Orlando
There are several farmers' markets in the Orlando area selling a wide variety of local seasonal produce such as tomatoes, Zellwood corn, blueberries and, best of all, strawberry onions, which are grown in the strawberry fields off-season and have a sweet flavour lightly perfumed with strawberry. These markets are increasing in popularity and more are opening over a wider area.

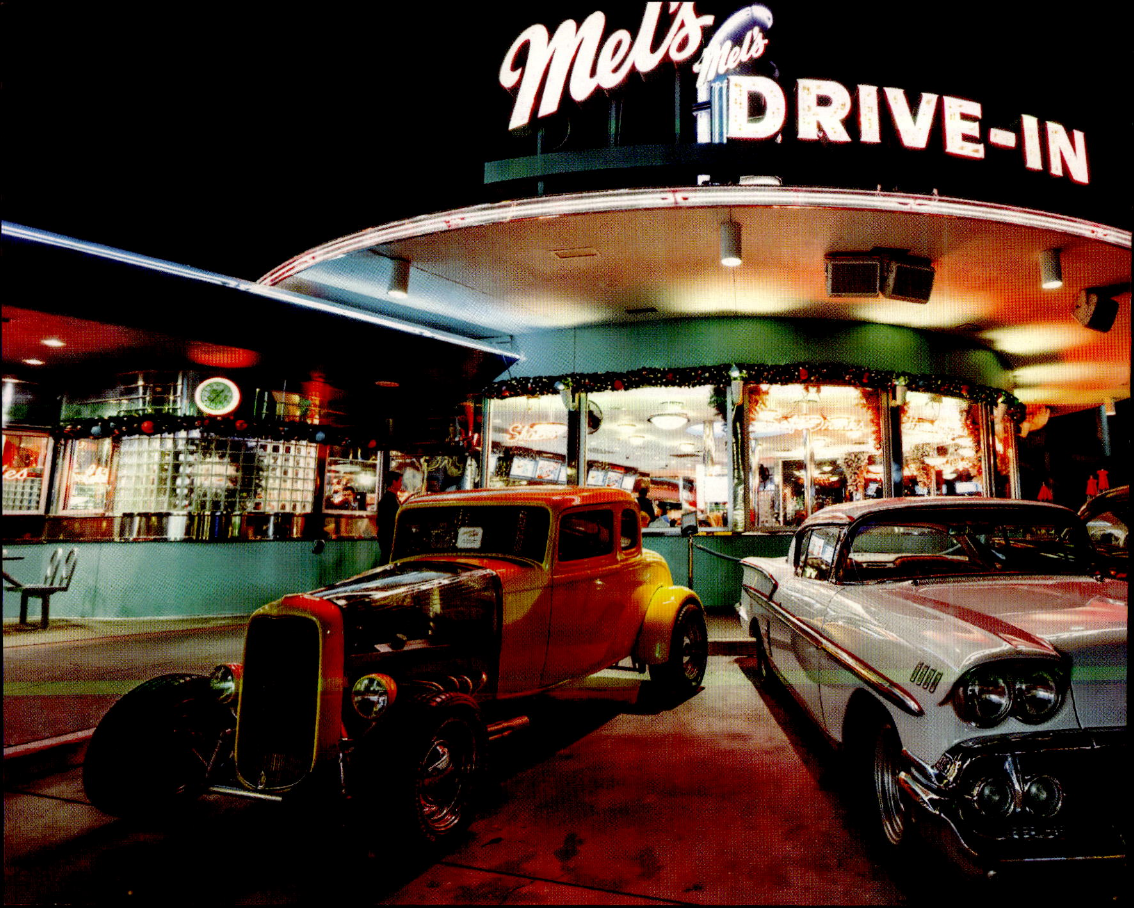
Mel's
Mel's
DRIVE-IN

OPPOSITE:

Mel's Drive-In
Located in Universal Studios, Mel's features great 1950s-style Americana and serves classic American diner food such as burgers, fries, milkshakes and root beer floats.

LEFT:

Universal Studios
The Amazing Adventures of Spiderman ride is one of many in Universal Studios Islands of Adventure section. Rather than being a rollercoaster, the experience is a motion-based 3D dark ride that features a virtual 123m (400ft) fall.

179

Hogwarts Railway, Universal Studios

Part of the Wizarding World of Harry Potter, the Hogwarts Express is in an area of the park based on the books by JK Rowling. Visitors can enjoy a pint of butterbeer in the Leaky Cauldron, buy an interactive wizard's wand from Ollivander's Wand Shop, get a Death Eater mask in Knockturn Alley, visit Diagon Alley, and get involved in any number of other magic-related activities.

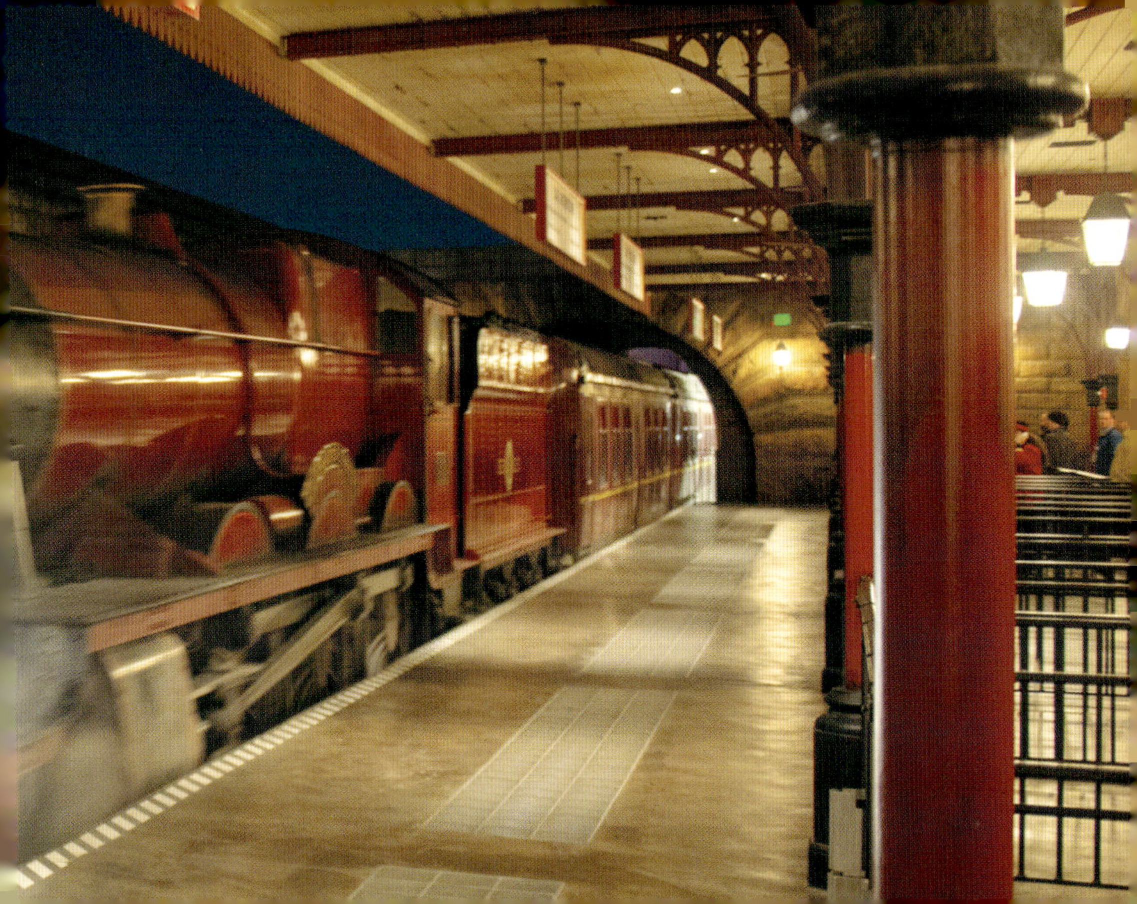

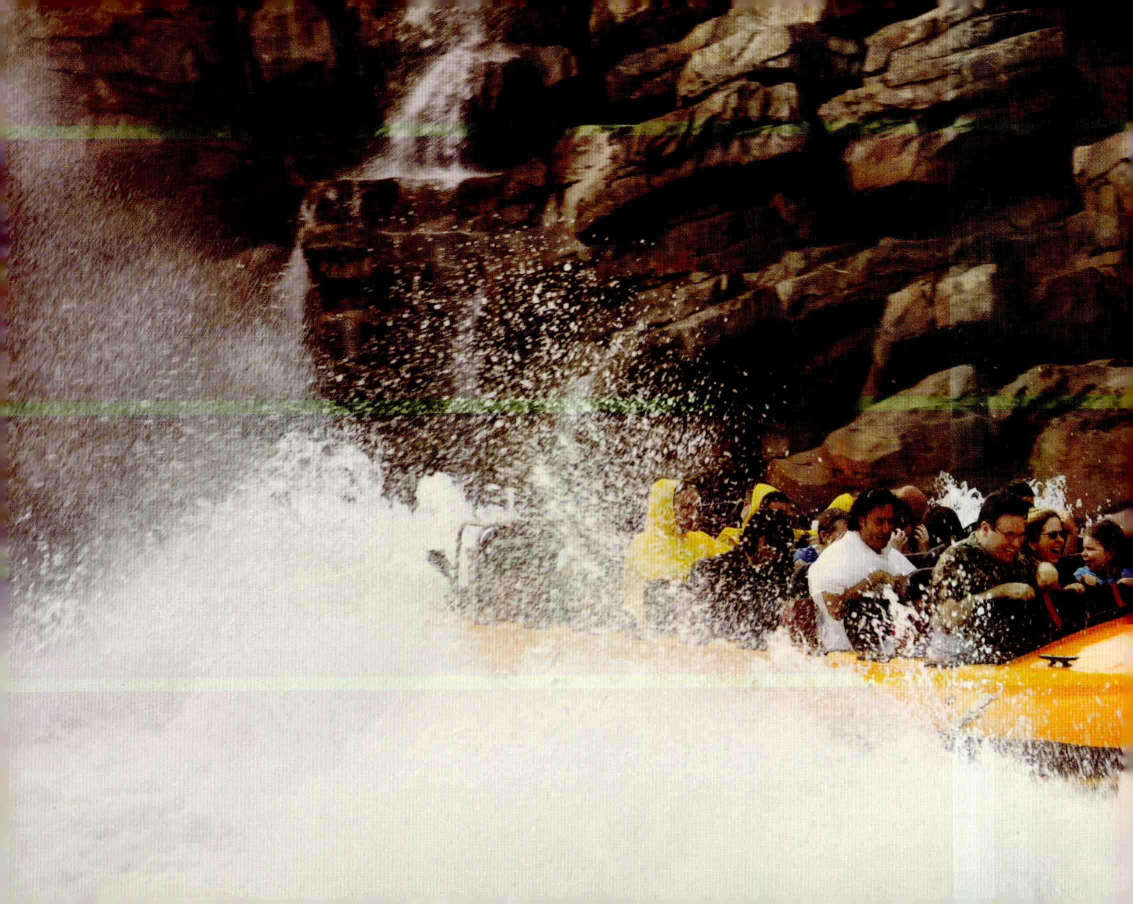

Jurassic Park River Adventure Ride, Universal Studios

When built, the ride's 26m (85ft) drop was the largest of any water ride in the world. Based on the Michael Crichton books and films, this ride covers a large area and remains a firm favourite with park visitors.

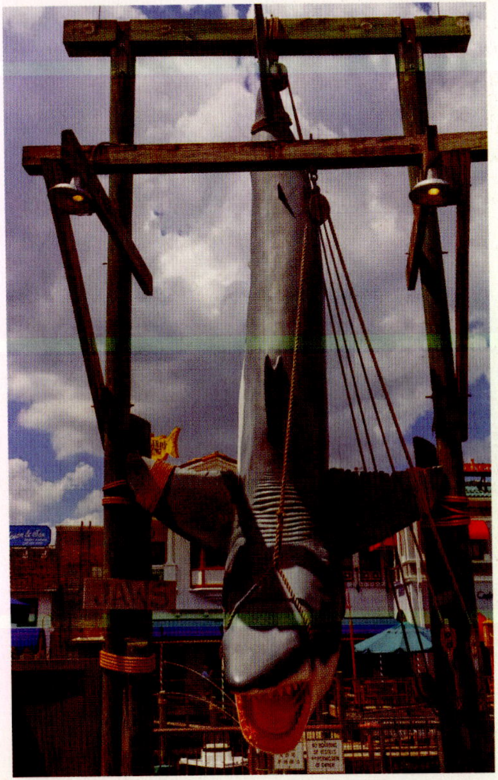
JAWS

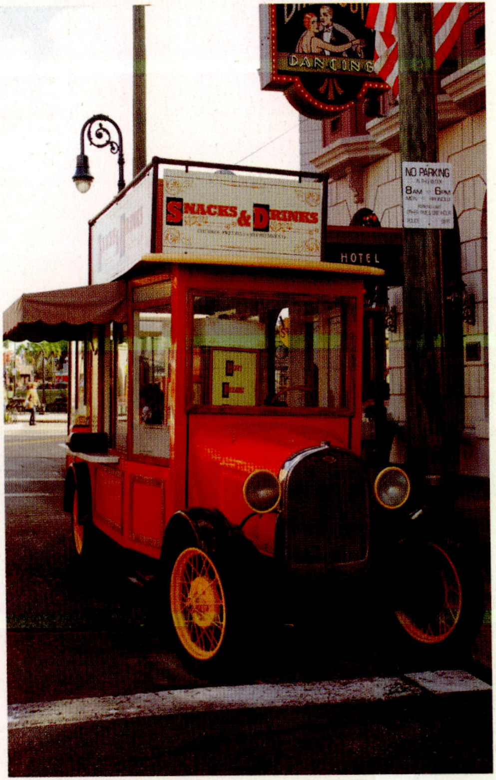
DANCING
SNACKS & DRINKS
HOTEL
NO PARKING
8AM 6PM

OPPOSITE LEFT:
Jaws ride, Universal Studios
One of the older but still popular rides, Jaws allows visitors to be menaced by a giant animatronic shark and live to tell the tale.

OPPOSITE RIGHT:
Antique food truck, Universal Studios
Selling anything from turkey legs to popcorn, these food trucks allow park visitors to get a snack without having to go through a crowded restaurant visit.

LEFT:
Blues Brothers, Universal Studios
Jake and Elwood do five shows a day and you can just stroll by or stop and watch a whole set.

ABOVE:
Walt Disney World Resort, Orlando
The story goes that Walt Disney was offended by a member of the Budweiser beer dynasty at a party in St Louis, Missouri, held to celebrate Disney's decision to build his new amusement park there. The next day, Disney left St Louis and started looking seriously at Orlando, and never looked back.

OPPOSITE:
Magic Kingdom Park, Walt Disney World
Magic Kingdom is the most popular theme park in the world. It's based on the original Disneyland in California and was the first of the four Orlando parks to open. It is divided into six themed 'lands': Fantasyland, Frontierland, Adventureland, Main Street USA, Tomorrowland and Liberty Square.

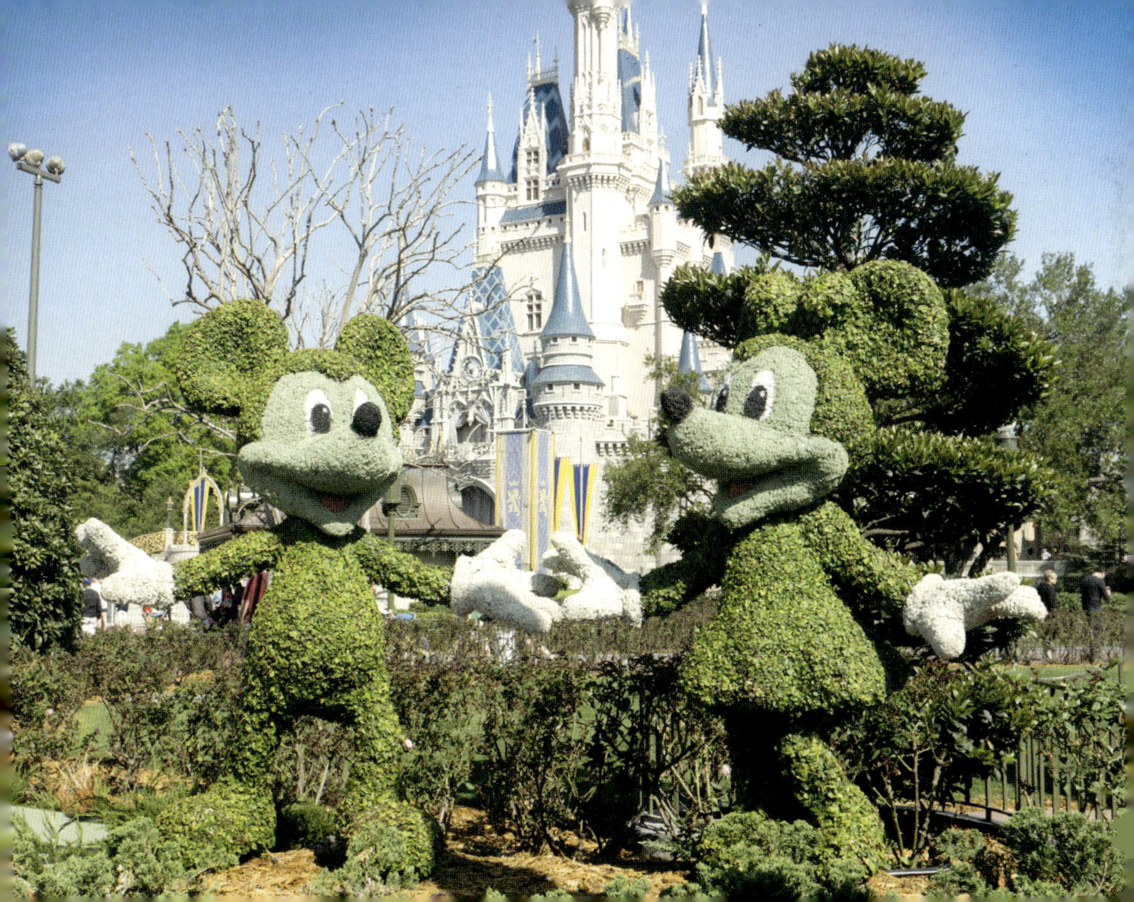

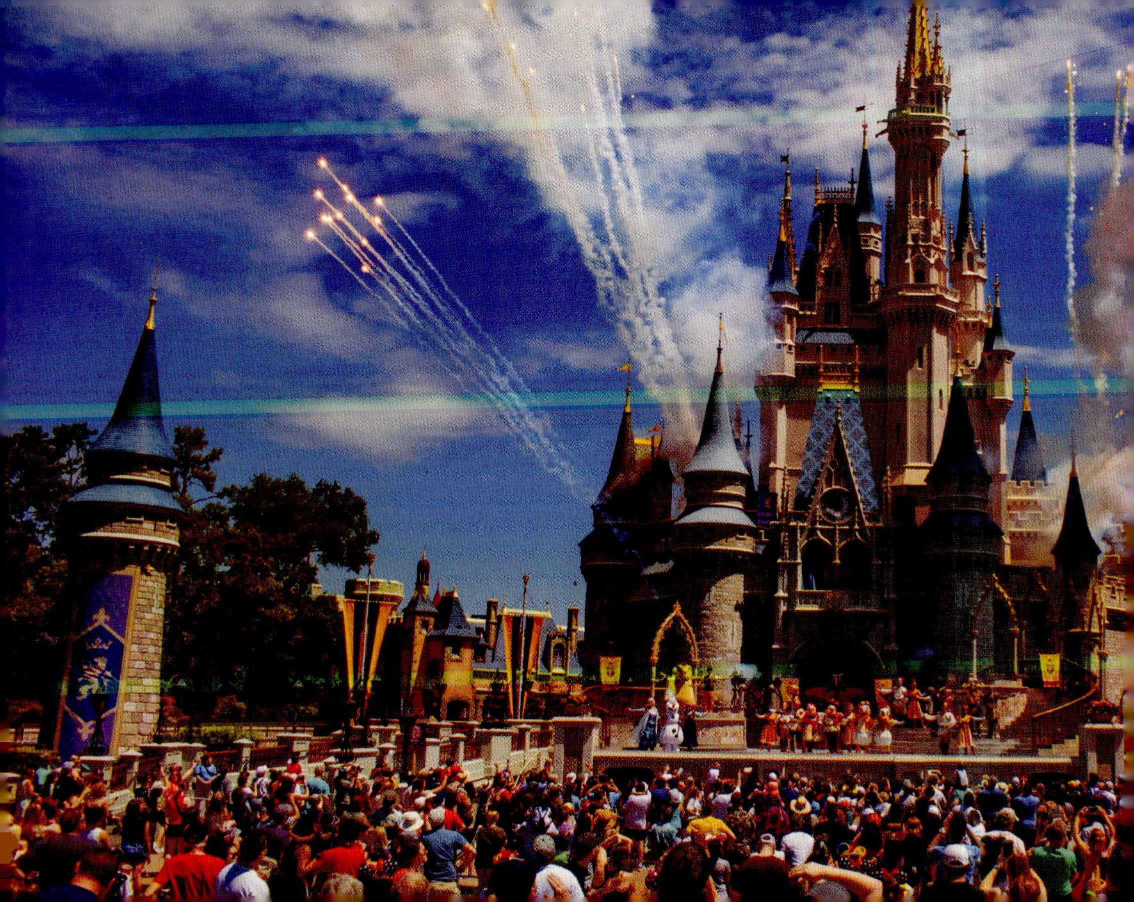

LEFT:
Mickey's Royal Friendship Fayre
Located in Main Sreet, this stage show stars Mickey Mouse and other classic Disney characters performing acts associated with the films they feature in.

ABOVE:
Bay Lake Tower, EPCOT
Part of Disney's Contemporary Resort, this hotel has pools, spas, bars and restaurants. EPCOT stands for 'Experimental Prototype Community of Tomorrow'.

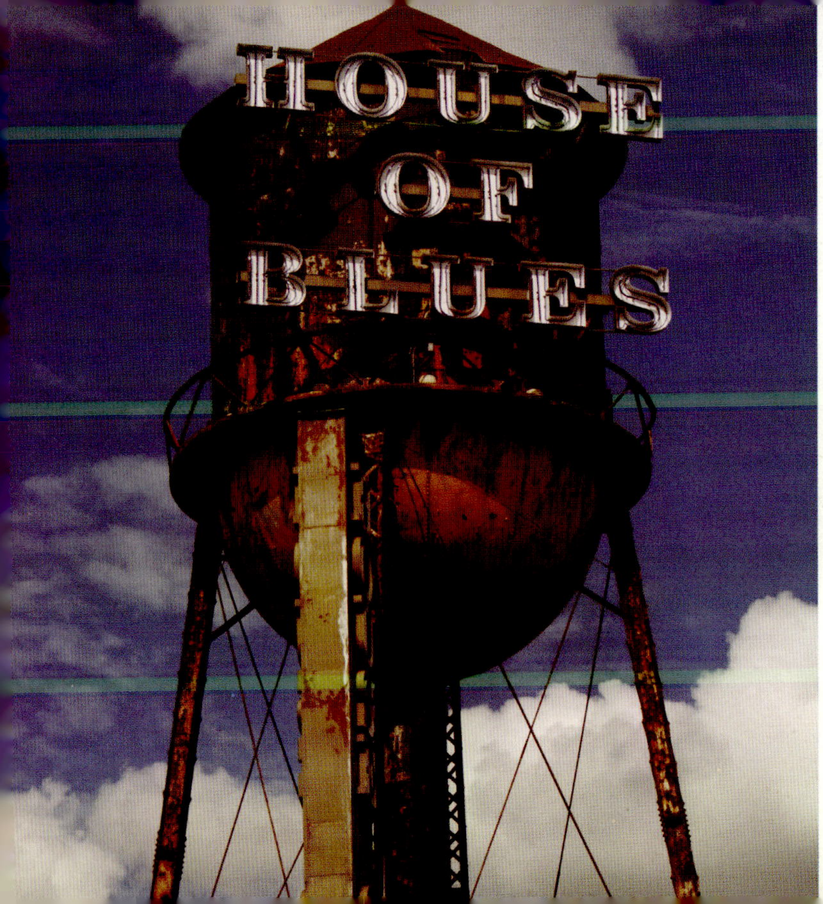
HOUSE
OF
BLUES

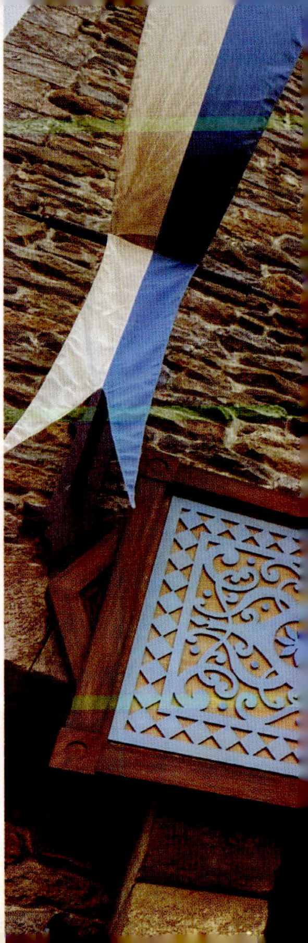

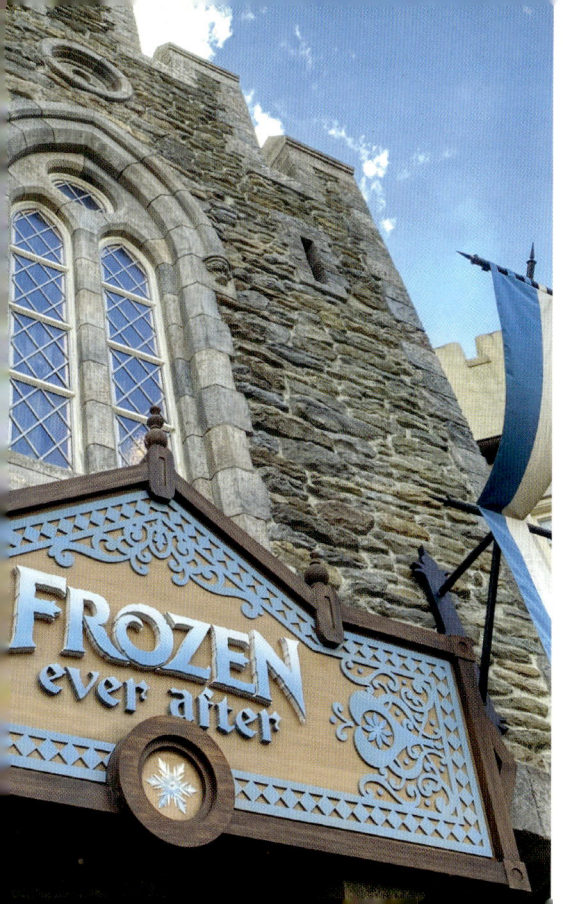

OPPOSITE:

House of Blues (HOB)
Set in Disney Springs, HOB is a concert venue as well as a bar and restaurant. It features southern-style food and a Sunday Gospel Brunch with live music.

LEFT:

Frozen Ever After
This ride is located in EPCOT and is based on the movie *Frozen*. Visitors take a voyage on an old Norwegian boat through the land of Arendelle.

ABOVE:

Disney characters
Mickey and Minnie on take to the stage with Goofy and Donald Duck in the Magic Kingdom.

RIGHT:
Main Street, Walt Disney World
The first thing visitors see when they enter the Magic Kingdom is a street based on 19th-century America, with horse-drawn vehicles and an old-fashioned barber shop, bakery and cinema.

OPPOSITE:
Band, Fairytale Castle, the Magic Kindgom
The Fairytale Castle is based on multiple real European castles and is one of the symbols of the Disney company, along with Mickey Mouse and other classic characters. It was finished in 1971, before being renovated in 2020 in honour of the 50th anniversary of the film *Cinderella*.

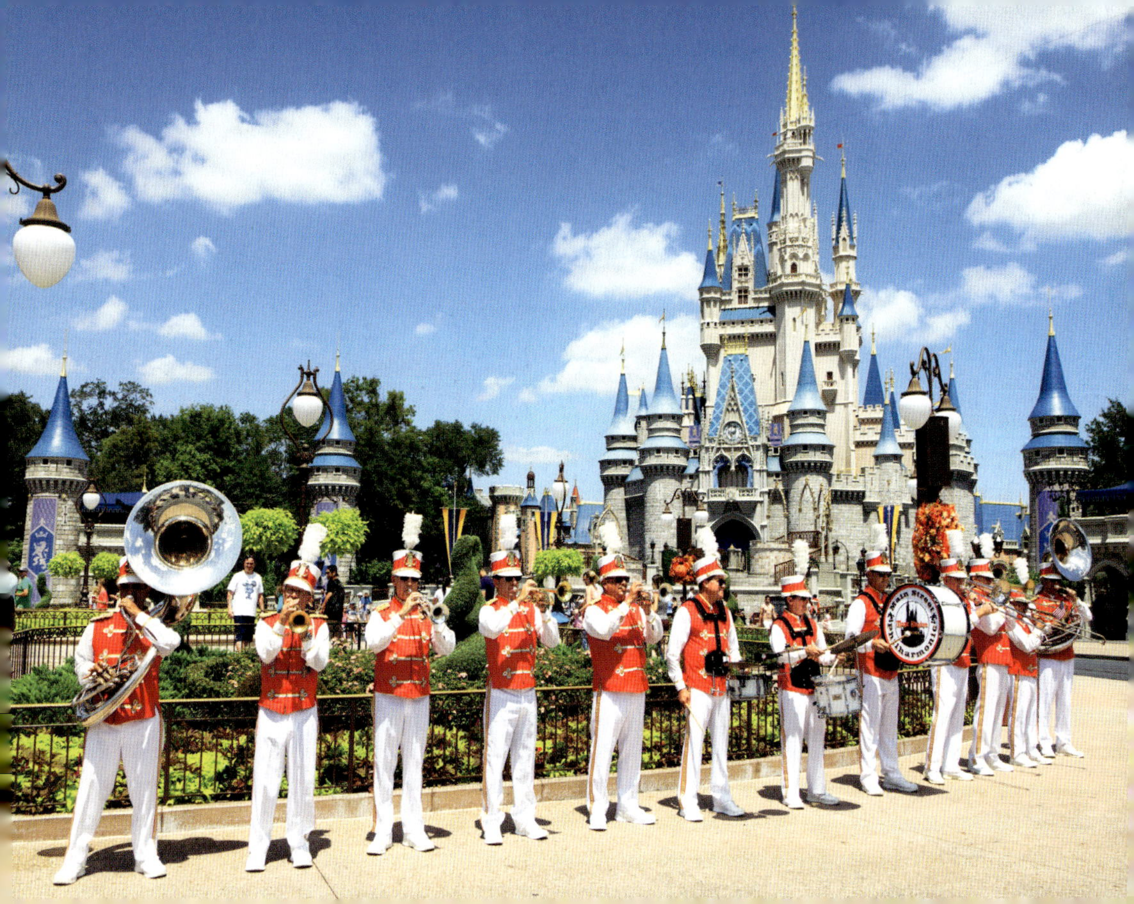
Main Street

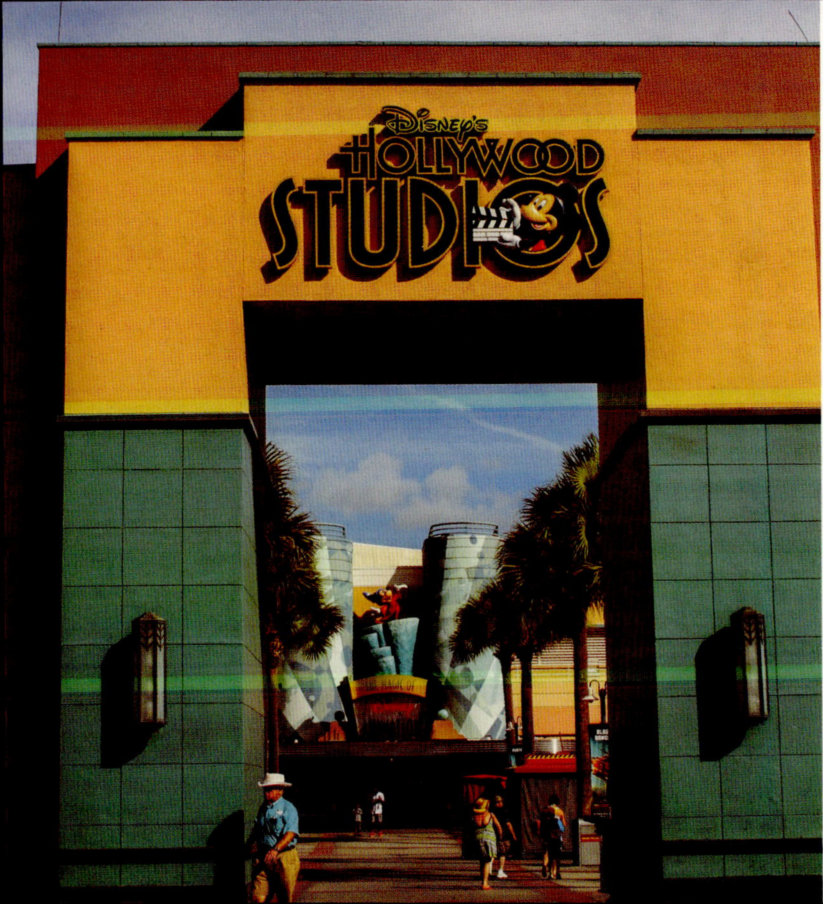
Disney's
HOLLYWOOD
STUDIOS
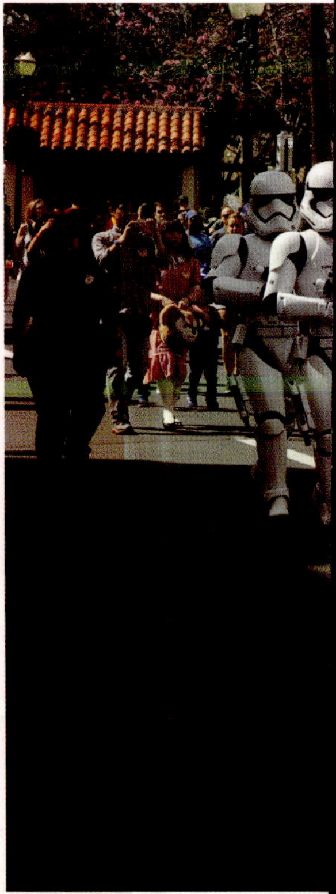

ALL PHOTOGRAPHS:
Disney Hollywood Studios

Opening in 1989 as Disney MGM Studios Park, Disney Hollywood Studios was the third of the four Disney theme parks to open. Originally opened as a functioning production and animation studio as well as an entertainment park, the production facilities have been closed and the space they took up used for new attractions. The MGM branding was removed in 2008.

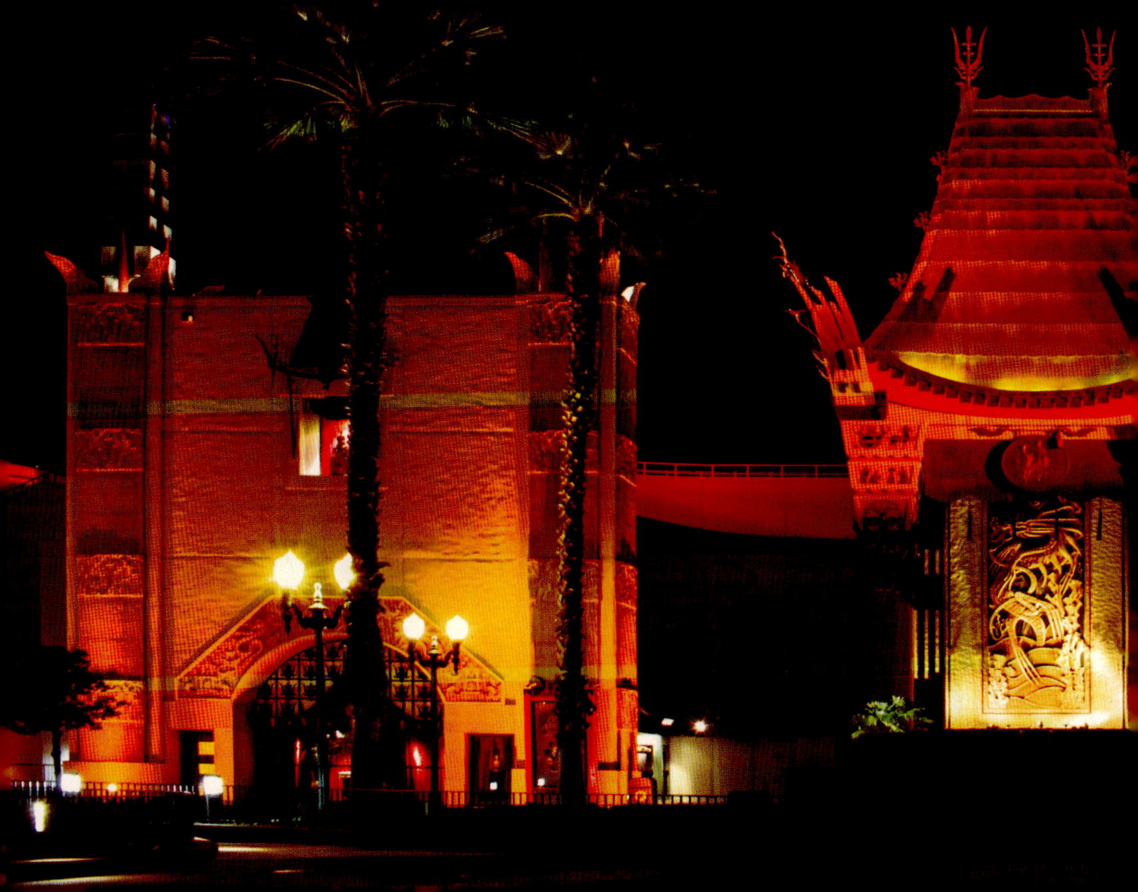

Chinese Theater, Hollywood Studios
Walt Disney put what he called 'weenies' into his theme parks, specific landmarks to keep you on a certain path. The Chinese Theater is the Hollywood Studios 'weenie' that leads you further into the park. It is built as a copy of the original Grauman's Chinese Theater, opened in Los Angles in 1927. One reason the Disney version is so authentic-looking is that they used the actual blueprota of the original to construct it.

Roller Coaster, Hollywood Studios

Themed as the Rockin' Roller Coaster featuring the band Aerosmith, this ride accelerates from 0–96 km/h (0-60mph) in 2.8 seconds, letting people on it experience 5G – more than an astronaut on the Space Shuttle does on launch. It goes through three inversions and multiple stops and loops and is loosely themed as if the riders are touring G Force Records and run into Aerosmith doing a recording session.

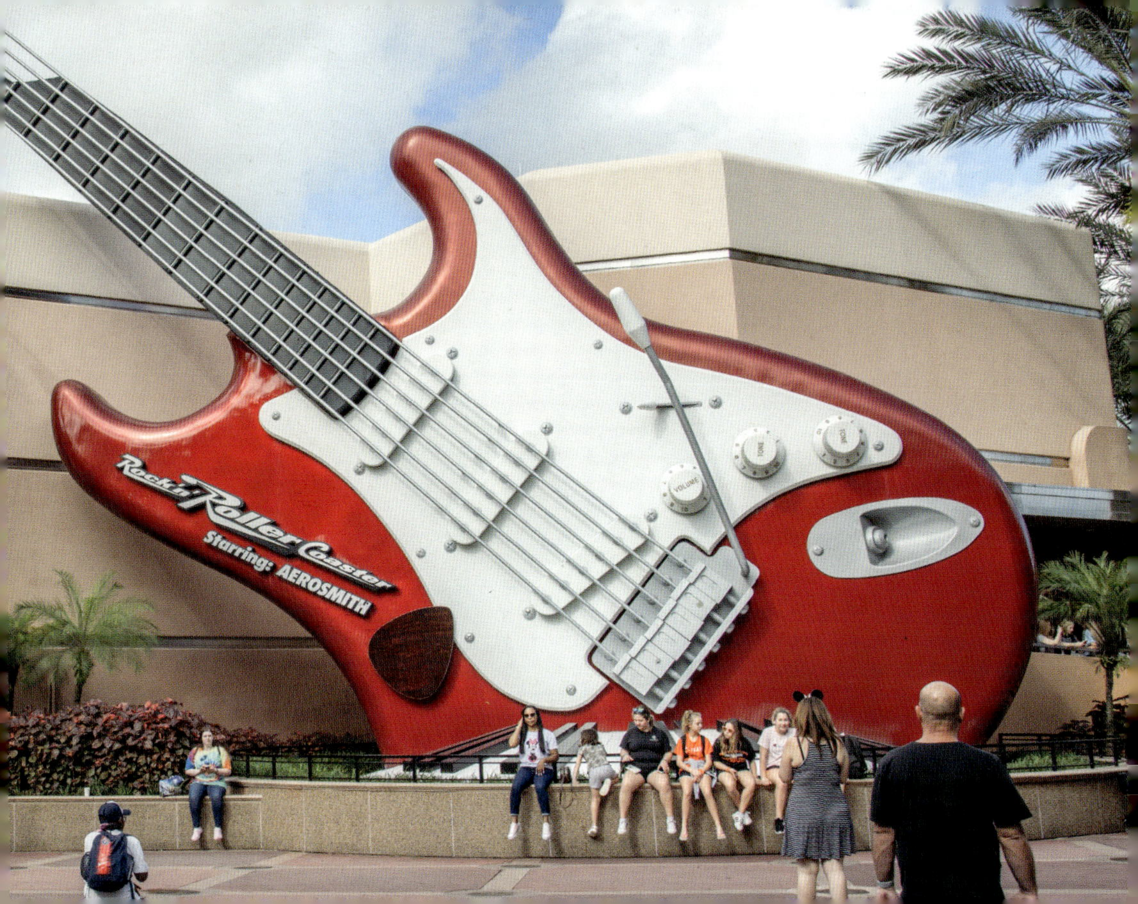
Rock'n' Roller Coaster
Starring: AEROSMITH
VOLUME
TONE
TONE

ABOVE:

Beauty and the Beast, Walt Disney World
Part of Fantasyland, the *Beauty and the Beast* show is an interactive telling of the classic story filtered through the lens of the Disney animated film, including Lumiere the perky candlestick.

RIGHT:

New Star Wars Galaxy's Edge, Hollywood Studios
Opened in 2019 simultaneously in both the Florida and California parks, this attraction features rides and merchandise based on the George Lucas films.

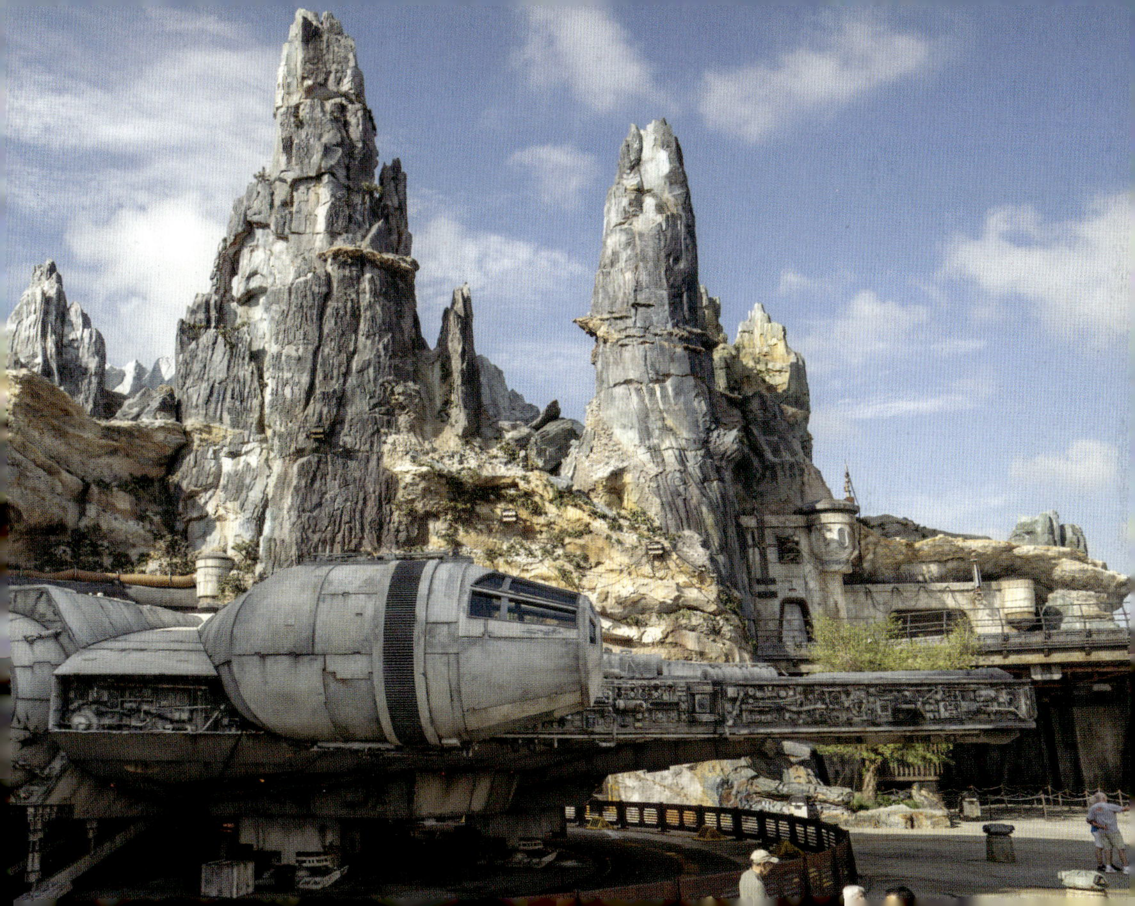

ALL PHOTOGRAPHS:
SeaWorld, Orlando
SeaWorld is an independent park in southwest Orlando that features a marine zoological theme for its attractions and rides. It is divided into three areas, SeaWorld, Discovery Cove and Aquatica. Visitors can come face to face with a giant black grouper (behind glass) and see many exotic creatures in its aquarium-style exhibitions.

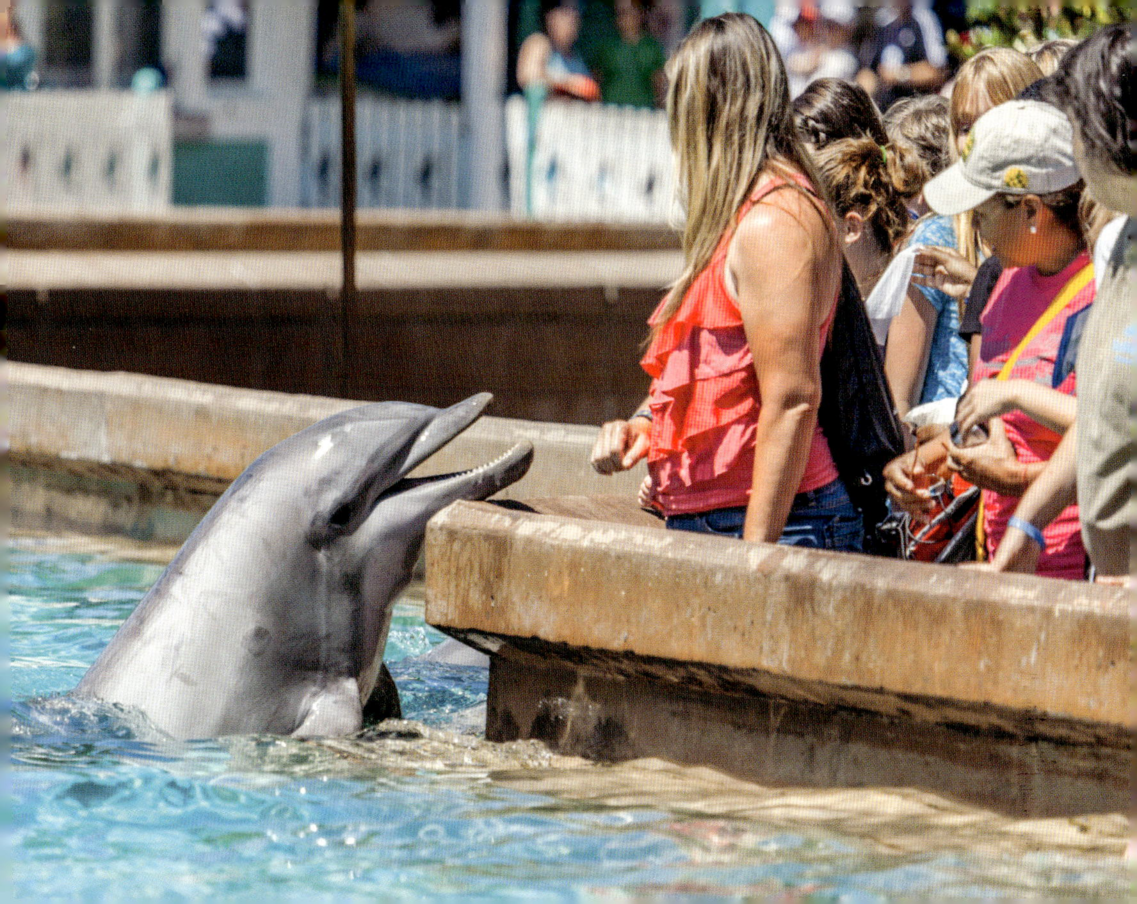

ALL PHOTOGRAPHS:
SeaWorld attractions
Among many other animals, visitors can see killer whales strut their stuff in an arena setting, though this has been made much more animal friendly and safer over the past 20 years. Other attractions at the park include roller coasters.

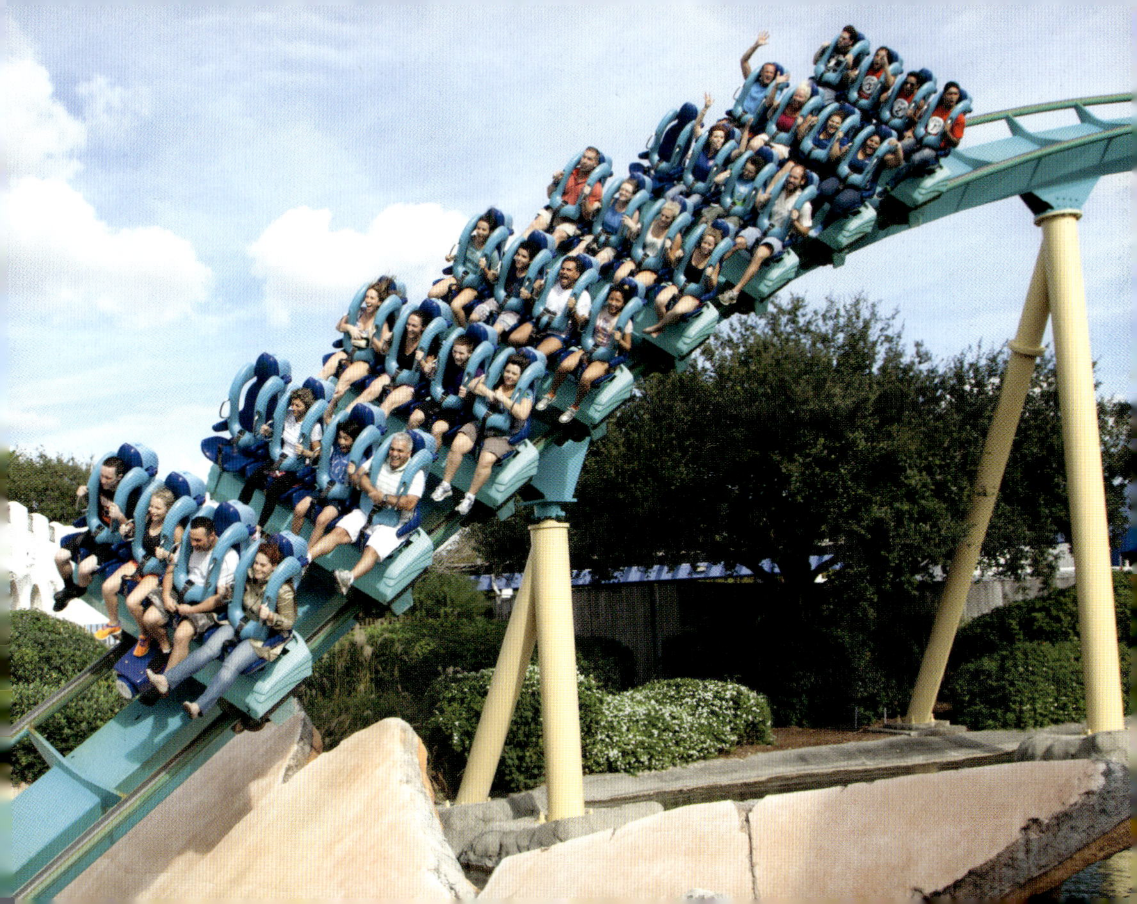

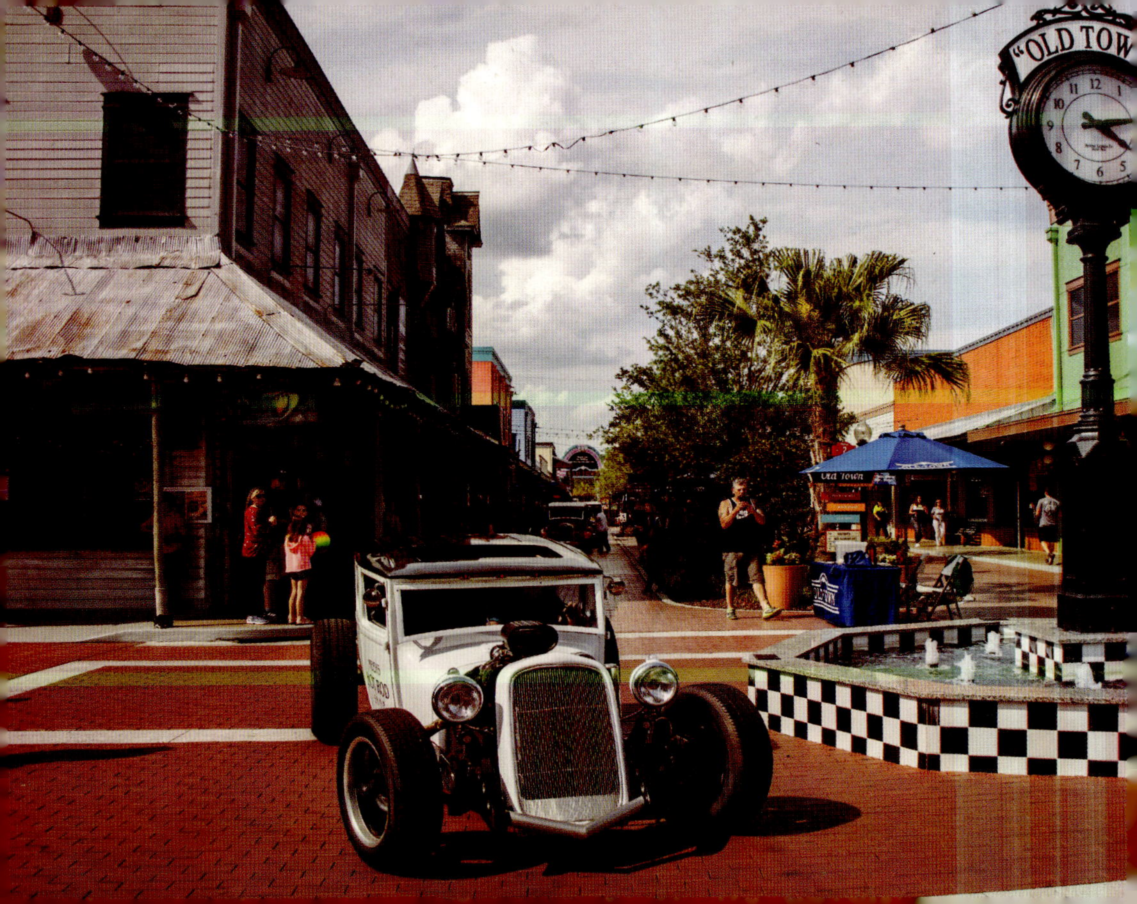
"OLD TOW
Old Town

LEFT:

Old Town Kissimmee Saturday Car Cruise
The car cruise is a regular feature in Kissimmee, the old cattle and citrus town south of Orlando and near to the Disney parks. Private owners of vintage cars and hot rods cruise the main street.

ABOVE:

Old Town Kissimmee Main Street at night
Lined with shops, bars and restaurants, Main Street offers an alternative nightlife to attractions around the parks.

207

GIFT

Jungle Falls Gift Shop, Kissimmee

The Orlando area is home to more souvenirs, T-shirts, trinkets and gift shops than possibly anywhere else. Even the grocery stores and chemists near the parks have branded items for sale. Jungle Falls Gift Shop is one of the larger of the out-of-park souvenir shops.

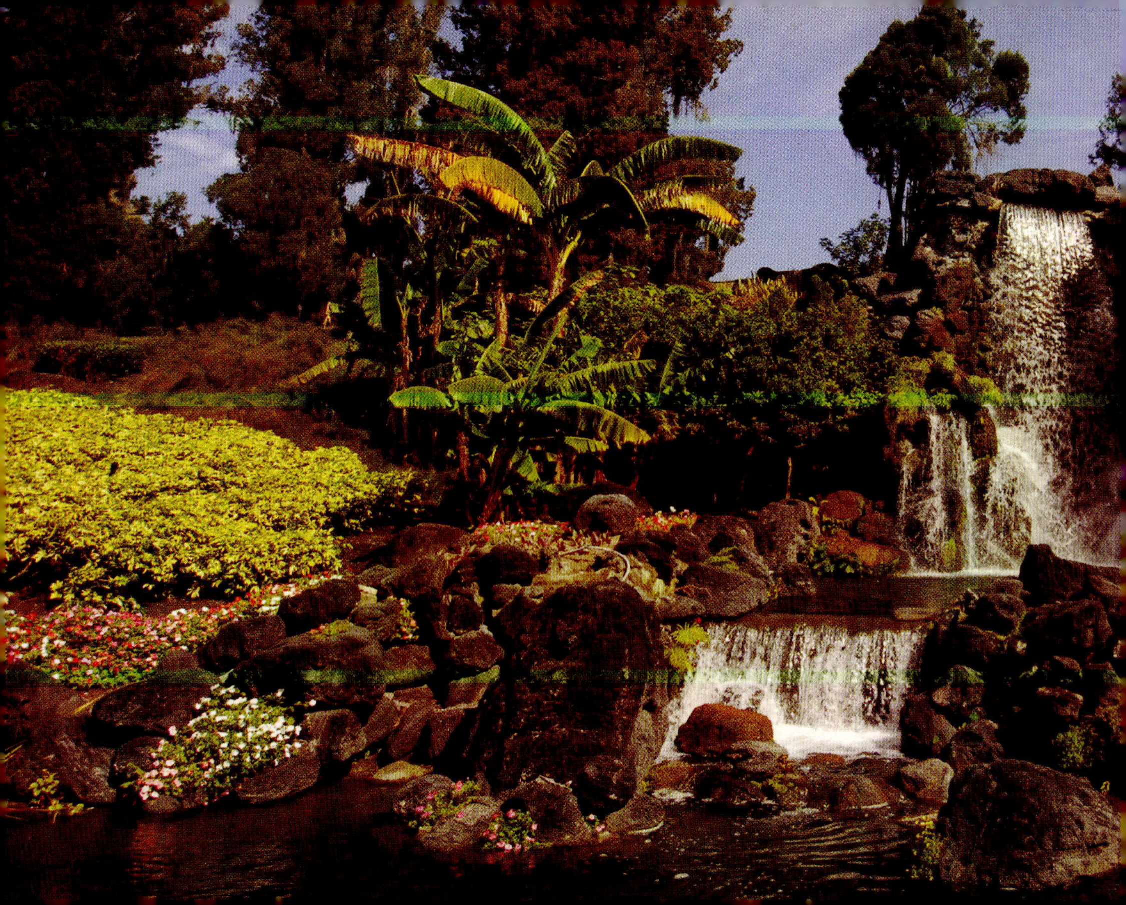

Waterfall at Cypress Gardens, Winter Haven
This leafy waterfall is part of the Cypress Gardens theme park, a short drive out of Orlando. It was actually Florida's first theme park, opening in 1936. Still operational today, despite a few closures along the way, it's very pretty spot. Parts of it can be rented for weddings and events. Dick Pope, who originally opened this park, was known as 'the father of Florida tourism'.

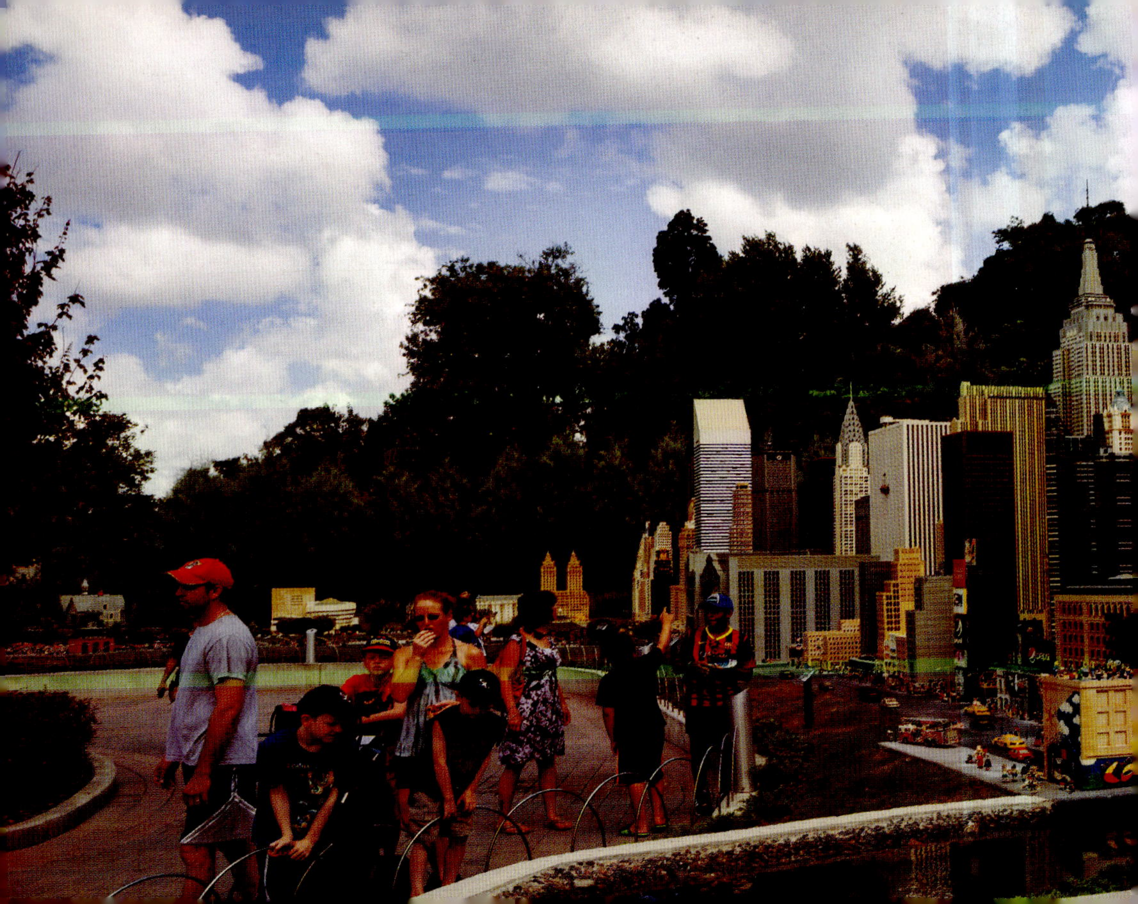

Legoland, Cypress Gardens, Winter Haven
About 45 minutes from Orlando and the same from Tampa, Legoland has rides, shows and other attractions and is obviously very much geared to children, as is the original in Denmark. It covers 60 hectares (150 acres) and is also a water park and botanical gardens.

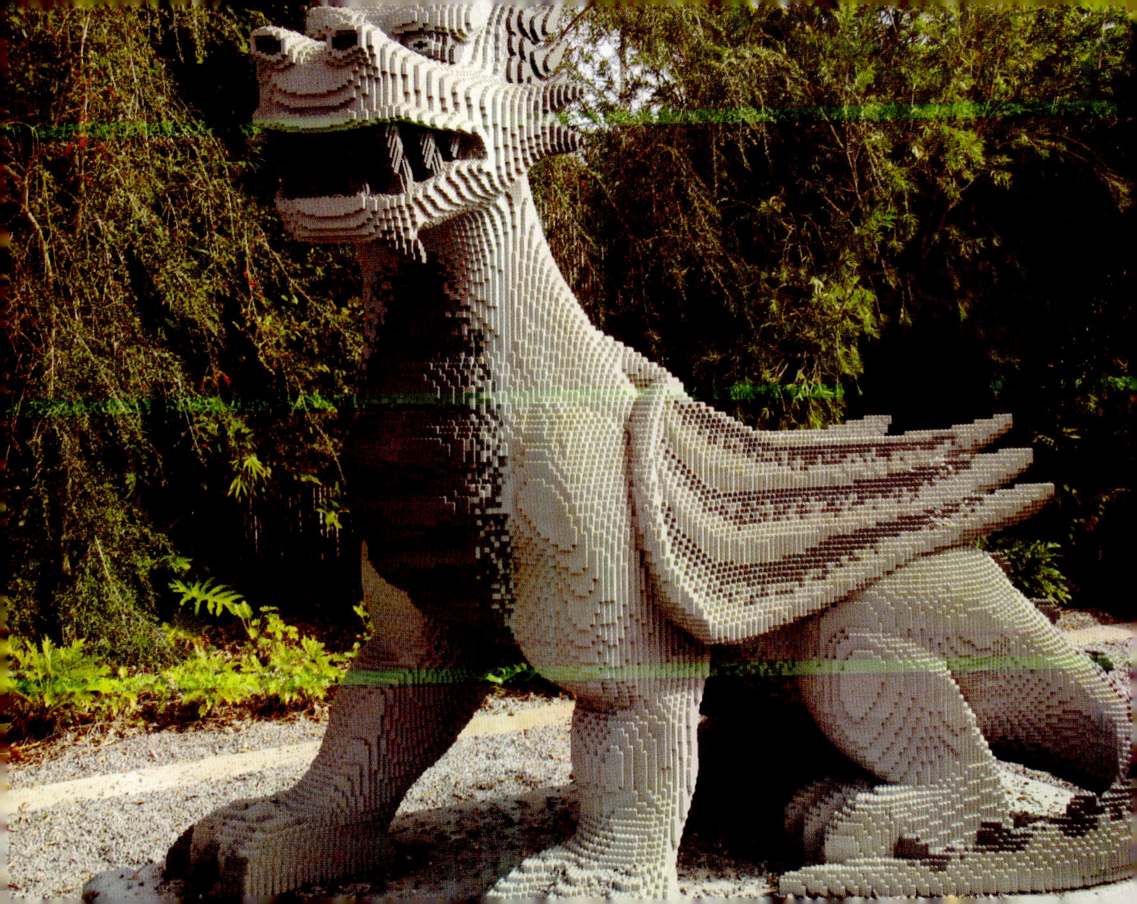

ALL PHOTOGRAPHS:
Legoland Florida
This park is the second-largest Legoland in the world, after Legoland Windsor in the UK. It features over 50 rides, shows and attractions. The park incorporates three separate hotels for overnight visitors. A separately ticketed Peppa Pig park opens in 2022.

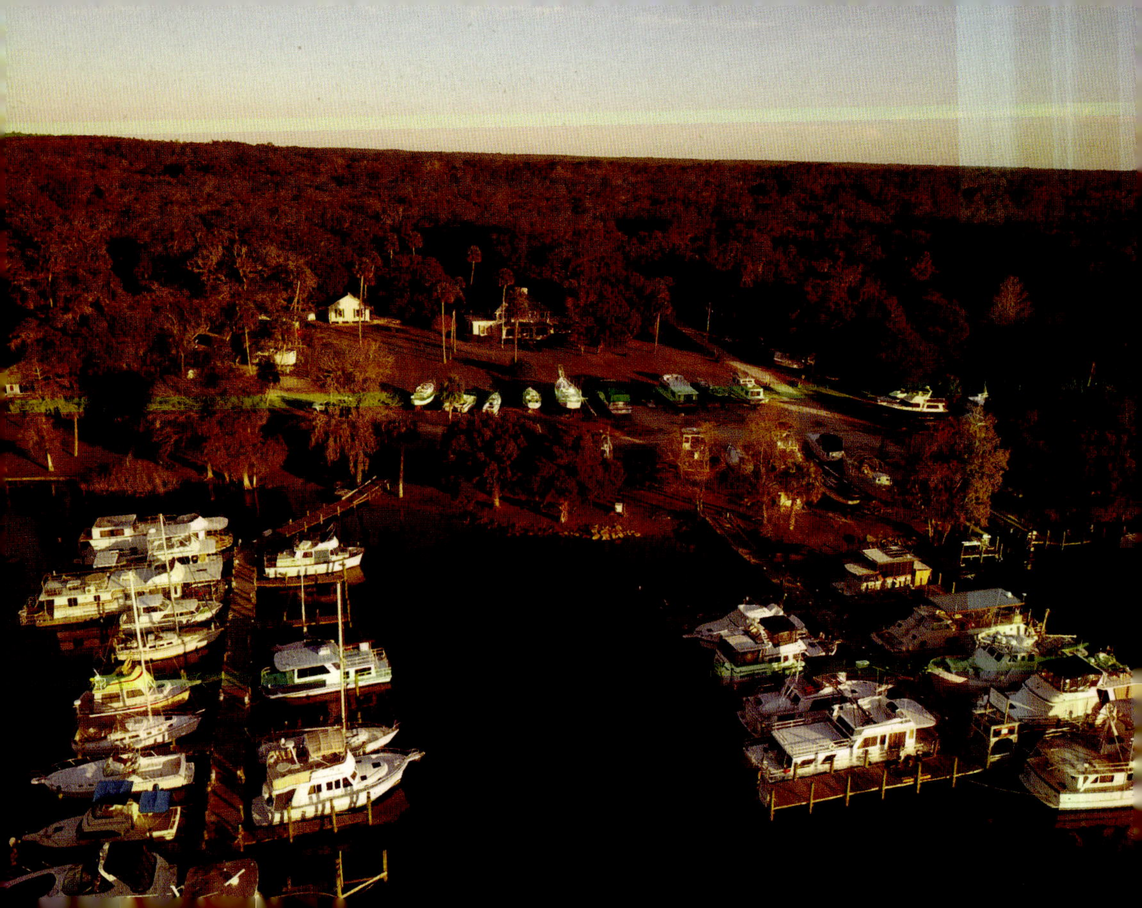

ALL PHOTOGRAPHS:
Ocala, Orlando

Ocala is a small city about an hour's drive north of Orlando. It is surrounded by beautiful countryside, including Silver Springs State Park and the Crystal River, where the original Tarzan films and *The Creature From The Black Lagoon* were filmed. The Ocala area is still quite rural and local produce can be sourced from farmers's markets (right). Nearby Ocala National Forest (opposite) is an unspoiled spot.

ABOVE:
Paddleboarding, Ocala
The Crystal River runs through Silver Springs State Park and allows visitors to paddleboard and canoe its waters, but they must watch out for the many alligators that flourish there.

RIGHT:
Ocala National Forest
Ocala National Forest is the second-largest in the state and the oldest national forest east of the Mississippi River. It has over 600 natural lakes and ponds and is an important filter for the Florida Aquifer. The US Navy's Pinecastle Bombing Range is located in the forest and live munitions are tested there with the Navy dropping thousands of bombs a year.

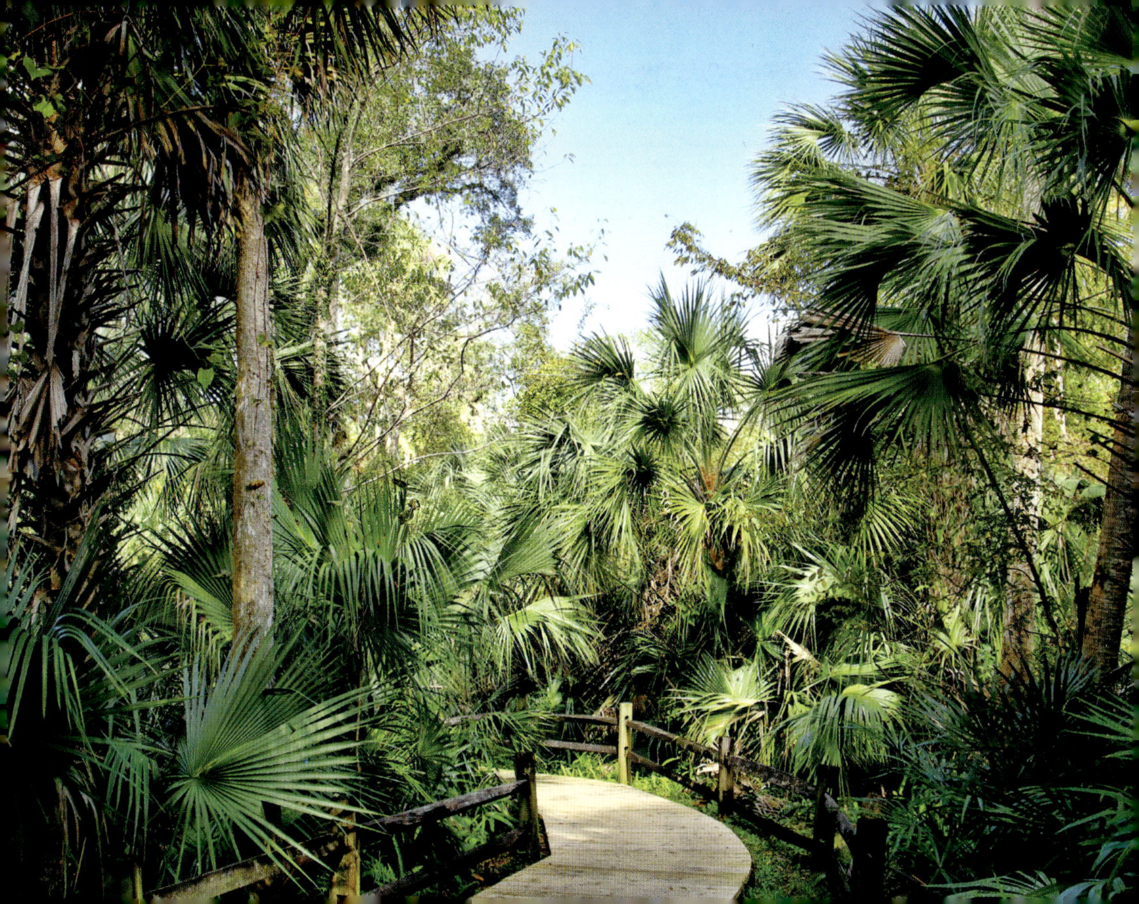

WINE BAR

OPPOSITE AND LEFT:
Sanford Historic District
Sanford lies at the head of the St John's River and its historic downtown features many architectural styles, including Craftsman, Prairie and Queen Anne. There are many bars, restaurants, craft breweries and other stops for visitors to enjoy.

ABOVE:
Cruise ship, Port of Sanford
Visitors can take a cruise on Lake Monroe or on the St John's River while enjoying live music and on board dining.

RIGHT:
Central Florida Zoo and Botanical Gardens
Formerly the Sanford Zoo and nestled in an natural wetland, this attraction has rhinos, leopards, monkeys, a Florida black bear, exotic birds and a reptile collection.

OPPOSITE:
Monroe Harbor Marina, Sanford
Monroe Harbor Marina acts as a base for cruises on the lake or the St John's River, the longest river in the state which, unusually, flows north.

Picture Credits

Alamy: 23 & 24 bottom both (Findlay), 29 (Franck Fotos), 38 bottom & 40 both (Jeffrey Isaac Greenberg), 41 (Ruth Peterkin), 46 (Torontonian), 48 left (Littleny), 48 right (John Kellerman), 49 (Angelo Cavalli), 50 left (Felix Stensson), 53 (Ian Dagnall), 68 (Ron Busrick), 70 (Terry Kelly), 78 (Katharine Andriotis), 80/81 (Aerial Archives), 103 top (M Timothy O'Keefe), 103 bottom (Renee McMahon), 104 (James L Peacock), 114 bottom (Sally Weigand), 120 (Lorne Chapman), 128 (WaterFrame), 129 (ArteSub), 134/135 (Ian Dagnall), 146 (Yvette Cardozo), 147 (parkerphotography), 148 (James Schwabel), 149 left (Laperruque), 149 right (Carmen Alex), 150 (Carl DeAbreu), 159 (Laperruque), 162/163 (Joe Quinn), 164 (Ian G Dagnall), 170 (McPhoto/Bachmann), 171 (imac), 175 (Tim E White), 187 (ShootingCompany), 189 (Horizon International Images), 193 (Findlay), 203 (RSBPhoto1), 206 (Shine-a-light), 207 (Ian Dagnall), 208/209 (MiraMira), 210/211 (MacDonald Photography), 217 (Ron Buskirk), 220 right (Bill Bachmann), 221 (Allan Hughes)

Dreamstime: 6 (Cheri Alguire), 7 (Sean Pavone), 10 (Picturemakersllc), 11 (Kevin Winkler), 12/13 (Sean Pavone), 16/17 (Barbara Smyers), 26 & 27 both (Walter Arce), 30 (Photogolfer), 31 (William Perry), 32 (Sean Pvone), 36 (Mira Agron), 38 top (Ruth Peterkin), 42 (Sergey Cherynaev), 43 (Fotoluminate), 44 (Beatrice Preve), 50 right (Fotoluminate), 51 (Ilfrede), 52 left (Alexander Elerian), 52 right (Benkrut), 54/55 (Curtis Smith), 56 (Linda Harms), 57 (Benkrut), 58 (Serenethos), 59 (Peter Leahy), 62 (Ppawel), 63 & 64 both (Jiawangkun), 65 (Ppawel), 66/67 (Christian Offenberg), 72/73 top (Giovanni Gagliardi), 72/73 bottom (Jon Bilous), 74 (Miroslav Liska), 75 (Jedikman), 76 (Ruth Peterkin), 77 (Whitlitzer), 82 (Viavaltours), 83 (Sean Pavone), 84/85 (Mike2focus), 86/87 (Sunburntblogger), 88/89 (Glenn Nagel), 90 (Viavaltours), 91 top (Felix Miziozinkov), 91 bottom (Dreammediapeel), 94 & 95 all (Khairil Junos), 96 right (Giovanni Gagliardi), 100 (Francocogoli), 101 (Fotoluminate), 105 (Jason Ondreicka), 106/107 (Fiskness), 110/111 (Loretta Risley), 112 (Jessamine), 114 top left (Vaclav Psota), 118 & 119 all (Giban59), 121 (Julienschiattino), 122 (Luca Nichetti), 123 top (Mtilghma), 123 bottom (Uhg1234), 124 top (Rajesh Pandit), 124 bottom (Joergspannhoff), 126/127 (William C Bunce), 130/131 (Jocrebbin), 132 (Ulf Nammert), 133 (Timgimages), 136/137 (Mark Bruch), 142 (Patricia A Hamilton), 143 (Jlabouyrie), 144 (Daniel Korzeniewski), 145 (Sherry Conklin), 154/155 (Izanbar), 156 (Ulf Nammert), 157 (Adeliepenguin), 158 (Ulf Nammert), 160 (Aiisha), 161 (Felix Miziozinkov), 167 (Kevin Ruck), 168/169 (Jon Bilous), 179 (Michael Gordon), 180/181 & 182/183 both (Jiawangkun), 184 left & 185 both (Solaisys13), 184 right (Jhernan124), 188 (Viavaltours), 190 left (Jai Mo), 190 right (Joni Hanebutt), 192 (Jiawangkun), 194 & 195 both (Jerry Coli), 196/197 (Viavaltours), 198/199 (Michael Gordon), 200 (Wisconsinart), 201 (Kevin Sokuroglu), 218 (Redwood8), 220 left (Sharonreed1)

Getty Images: 114 top right (Jeff Greenberg), 172 (Gina Pricope), 174, 176 & 177 all (Jeff Greenberg), 191 (Melvyn Longhurst)

Shutterstock: 8 (Christopher V Jones), 14 (Henryk Sadura), 15 (Fotoluminate LLC), 18 (Angela N Perryman), 19 (Sean Pavone), 20 (Shackleford Photography), 21 (Dave Allen Photography), 22/23 (Nick Fox), 24 top & 25 both (Sean Pavone), 28 (Edie Ann), 33 (Microfile.org), 34 (Ivan Cholakov), 35 (Manny DaCunha), 37 (Mike Kuhlman), 39, 45 & 47 all (travelview), 60 (YES Market Media), 61 (ByDroneVideos), 71 (Rotorhead 30A Productions), 79 top (Peter Titmuss), 79 bottom (Barnes Ian), 92 (Sean Pavone), 93 (Timothy OLeary), 96 left (Dylan Jon Wade Cox), 97 (Anna Katharina Meyer), 98/99 (mariakray), 102 (ESB Professional), 108/109 (William Eugene Dummitt), 113 (Danita Delimont), 115 (John Bilous), 116 (Anthony Ricci), 125 (Gagliardi Photography), 138 (EB Adventure Photography), 139 (Off Axis Production), 140 (Paul Harrison), 141 (Paul Brady Photography), 151 (Bertl123), 152/153 (Stacy Funderburke), 166 (Songquan Deng), 173 (ESB Professional), 178 (MontenegroStock), 186 & 202 both (Viaval Tours), 204 (dmitro2009), 205 (Erin Cadigan), 212/213 (Rob Hainer), 214 (Ritu Manoi Jethani), 215 (Joseph M Arseneau), 216 (Catherine Cornish), 219 (Rafal Michal Gadomski), 222 (KLiK Photography), 223 (Javier Cruz Acosta)

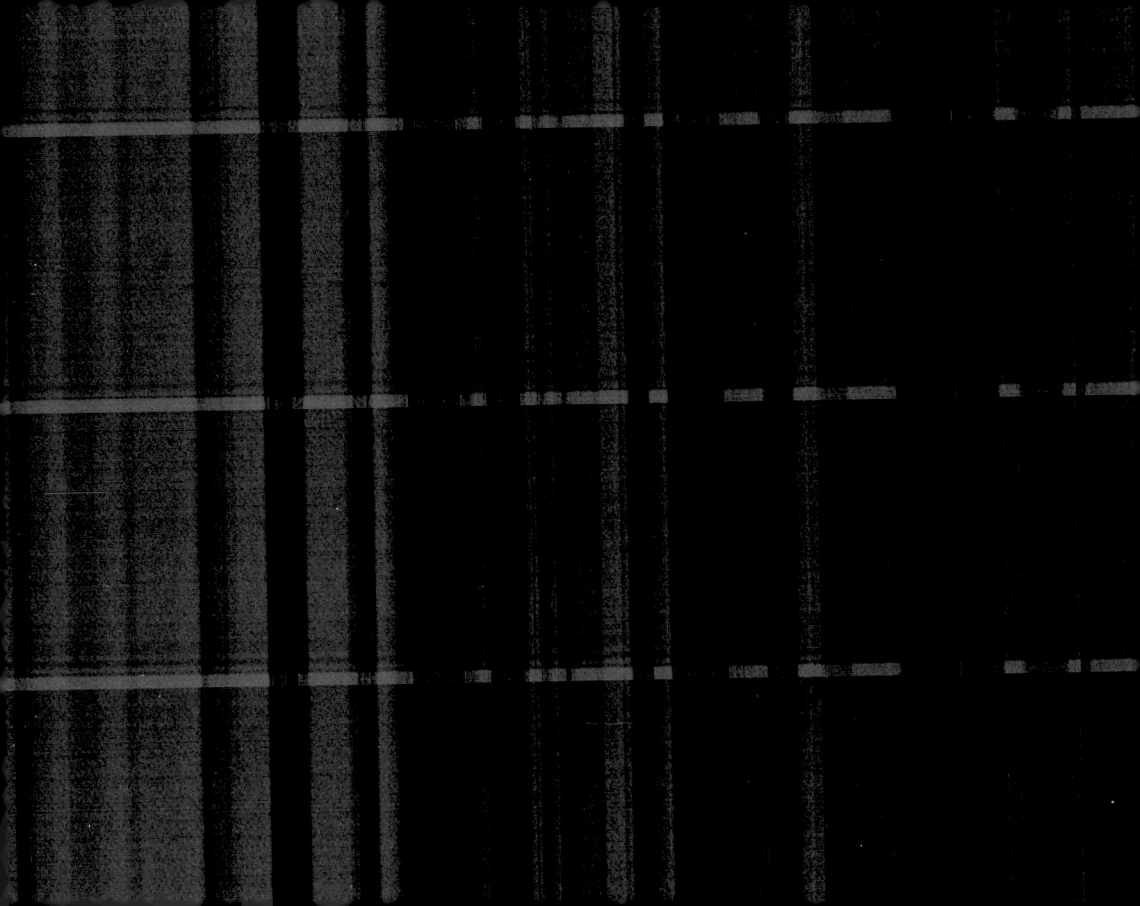